The Foodbirds

John Podmore

Many Happy Landings

Molly G. L. White

The Foodbirds

Flying for Famine Relief

THE STORY OF ONE OF THE
GREATEST MERCY AIRLIFTS THE WORLD HAS KNOWN

Molly O'Loughlin White

bmp

BOOKMARQUE
PUBLISHING
Minster Lovell · Oxfordshire

To 'Fat Albert' – 12,000,000 flying hours and 40 years young.
And to the 'Ascoteers' – the four Tactical Hercules Squadrons of the Lyneham Transport Wing –
whose dedication and selflessness inspired this story.

First published 1994

© Molly O'Loughlin White

ISBN 1-870519-24-8
(Limited Casebound Edition)

....

British Library Cataloguing in Publication Data

A catalogue record for this book is available from the British Library

Edited by T. C. Colverson
Typeset in 10½ on 12 point Garamond Book Condensed
by Bookmarque Publishing
Printed on Fineblade Smooth 115 gsm
Published by Bookmarque Publishing · Minster Lovell & New Yatt · Oxon
Printed and bound by Butler & Tanner Ltd · Frome · Somerset

FRONTISPIECE
LXX Squadron crew ready to board XV178 for a day's air-dropping at Derek Amba.
(Left to right) Ground engineer Sgt Bill Cork, Air Loadmaster Keith Jones,
flight engineer Master Engineer Doug Johnson, co-pilot Flt Lt Doug Maugham,
captain Flt Lt John Clements, navigator Flt Lt Doug Marsh.
Photo author

TITLE PAGE
Air-dropping at Derek Amba in the central Ethiopian highlands – XV178, one of RAF Lyneham's oldest inhabitants.
Photo Martin McWilliam

Contents

Acknowledgements

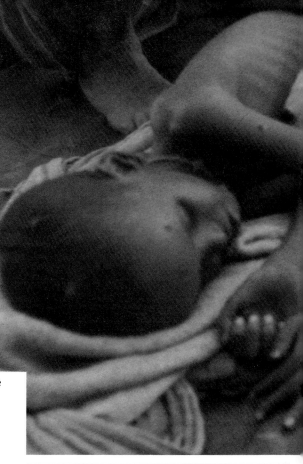

The four tactical squadrons of the Lyneham Transport Wing and support wings at Royal Air Force Lyneham.

47 Air Despatch Squadron, Royal Corps of Transport

The Ministry of Defence (Air)

The RAF Air Historical Branch

RAF Lyneham Public Relations and Station Magazine Editorial

The Relief and Rehabilitation Commission of Ethiopia

The Air Transport Wing LTG.61 of the West German Luftwaffe

The Polish Relief Helicopter Squadron

The Air Transport Wing of the Swedish Air Force

15th Wing Transport and Communications Command, Belgian Air Force

Canadian Forces Air Transport Group

Lockheed Aeronautical Systems Company

Mission Aviation Fellowship

Helimission of Switzerland

Air Botswana Cargo

Ethiopian Airlines

Southern Air Transport

Zimex Aviation

The International Committee of the Red Cross

The Lutheran World Federation, Sweden

World Vision

The many, many people who raided their photo albums and wrote to me.

BIBLIOGRAPHY

Transall – Engel der Lufte (Horst Walter/ Dietmar Plath)

Lockheed Hercules Francis K Mason

KEY TO ABBREVIATIONS

ADF	Automatic Direction Finding
AMSL	Air mean sea level
ASCOT	Air Support Command Operational Traffic
DME	Distance-measuring Equipment
DZ	Drop Zone
ETA	Estimated Time of Arrival
IFR	Instrument Flight Rules
NDB	Non Directional Beacon
QNH	Altimeter setting at mean sea level pressure
RRC	Relief and Rehabilitation Commission of Ethiopia
TAS	True Air Speed
VOR	Very High Frequency Omni-directional Radio Range
VFR	Visual Flight Rules
WAT	Weight, Altitude and Temperature

Introduction

"WE are here to assist the Ethiopian government, for purely humanitarian reasons. You have come to a land of sunshine and high altitude operations, where air traffic is purely procedural and honesty and integrity in the air and on the ground are crucial. There are many opportunities for low level VFR flying – but there is heat, there is turbulence – and birdstrikes are a major hazard.

"It is good fun flying – but you'll be hot, you'll be sticky, and flying in conditions you have never encountered before. From Assab you'll be lifting 42,000 pounds of grain at 40°C – very near the envelope for this aircraft. When you pull it off it won't want to come. Sometimes you'll be asked to park on a postage stamp and have to reverse before you can taxi. If you are not happy, then don't! We don't want wing tips bent."

The relief crew who had flown in on the resupply Hercules sat quietly in the Addis Ababa hotel room and listened to the briefing by Wing Commander David Guest, one of eight Wing Commanders who had each taken his turn as detachment commander of Operation Bushel, the contribution by the British Armed Forces to famine relief in Ethiopia during 1984-85. They had flown in to Bole Airport from RAF Lyneham in Wiltshire just two hours earlier and had already listened to dire warnings by the Medical Officer, of the water, the sun, the altitude and the local 'attractions'. At dawn tomorrow they would be airborne again on a first recce flight with an established crew, air-dropping grain on to some tiny drop zone surrounded by faulted volcanic mountains and gorges, or airlifting food from the Red Sea ports into a remote, stony, dusty airstrip. They were just one crew from the Lyneham Transport Wing who gave three weeks of their lives and skills delivering food, when a half pound of grain arriving on time meant the difference between death and existence, albeit a hard one, for many hundreds of thousands of people. The Hercules captain, Flight Lieutenant Bill Akister, had heard it all before. For him and a number of others it was a second time around.

This is the story of superb professionalism in the air coupled with compassion, and of the team spirit and enthusiasm of the airmen and soldiers who provided back-up. It is also the story of a unique international co-operation between aviators, some of them from opposing political regimes, practical, no-nonsense 'truckie' people of the air, getting together and sharing skills and training meant for war when hours saved meant lives saved. The three-point mutual support between the British Military Detachment, the Luftwaffe and the Polish Relief Helicopter Squadron which made air-dropping operations in country areas possible was, though small overall, a significant effort towards returning the country to its own socio-economic balance.

Over seventy per cent of the total food delivered by air for famine relief was either airlifted or air-dropped by the Royal Air Force – over 32,000 tonnes in all. It must be recognised that this was but a small amount in comparison with that delivered in road transport by the many relief organisations. But the big success story was the speed at which it reached so many hungry mouths.

When the call came no-one could fail to be disturbed by the human misery and deprivation, depicted on television screens the world over. Millions gave money – many others active help and their own time and skills, frequently struggling amidst chaos caused by political interference, amateurism (with the best will in the world), weather and terrain limitations beyond their control. The RAF contributed the expertise of the 'Ascoteers' (as the four Hercules transport squadrons dub themselves, after their singular call-sign 'ASCOT', Air Support Command Operational Traffic, which differentiates between purely military tactical aircraft and that of RAF transports, which frequently flew into civil airfields), logistics, cost-effectiveness and motivation. They gave a lead and example to many other military and civilian operators, sharing their skills and often providing a helping hand so that efforts by others could be turned from a losing battle into a success.

It is also a story of 'Fat Albert', the tough, tactical Lockheed C-130 – so christened by crews of the US Navy's formation aerobatic team, The Blue Angels, when their own Marine Corps support Hercules was equipped with eight rockets for a jet-assisted take-off (imagine! A jet propelled 'Herc'!) and given a display slot of its own. The name is still affectionately used by British servicemen who fly it and work with it to this day. This book tells too of the C-130s of other nations and of the dark, equally ungainly C-160 'Tralls' of the Luftwaffe and some of the many, many

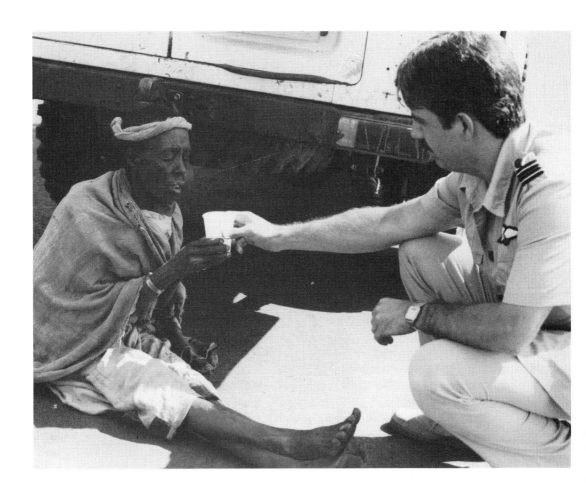

smaller aircraft, fixed-wing and rotor-bladed, which delivered those few pounds of food to someone who, but for their technical excellence, would not be alive today. Their pilots, crews and operators saw the haunting eyes of hunger, responded and did what they could, to the limits of their own particular aircraft.

Pragmatic 'truckie' crews do not talk about courage, a cool head or skill. They just get on with the job. But others who saw the selflessness with which they flew, hour after hour in extremely uncomfortable, often dangerous, conditions, will not forget their contribution. Before they left, they were the toast of Addis.

Good fun flying it may have been, but the commitment was absolute. As one RAF Herky pilot put it, simply: "It was by far the best thing I have ever done."

* * *

Twelve years of drought and one of the longest-running wars in the history of the world had decimated what is described in old guide books as a fertile land. Many millions of words have been written about famine in Ethiopia, and no doubt there will be many more. The problems of Africa do not disappear. There is the ever-present fear of drought, though by using modern technology and the natural resilience and ingenuity of the people some of the difficulties are being overcome. With the advent of rain and unprecedented amounts of foreign aid there were some considerable improvements. But only when there is continued peace and stability and the needs of ordinary people are not sacrificed to political aims will there be any hope for the future. What happened in Ethiopia could and did happen again, and continues to happen in many parts of Africa.

It was estimated that over seventy-eight per cent of Ethiopia's population of 42 million lived north of Addis Ababa where the drought hit hardest, diverse people with many tongues. No-one has, as yet, got around to rationalising the spelling of provinces, towns and country districts. On every map, in every document, it differs. I have endeavoured to keep to the spelling used in Ethiopian Airlines' maps and mostly adopted by the RAF. Any reader who remembers Shewa and Tigre provinces as Shoa and Tigrai, Makalle with two e's and one l, Gondar as Gonder, and so on, please bear with me. It will be noticed that the spelling varies widely on the maps and charts contributed by different operators.

The RAF mission was very aptly named 'Operation Bushell', though it was entirely co-incidental – in a chronological list of names which must not clash. It just came up, next on the list, though no-one quite knew why it was originally given two ls, perhaps influenced by the name of someone who happened to be passing or the quaint spelling of one whose task was to think up creative titles. It was officially decided it should be spelt with one l.

Crews and relief workers alike showed tremendous enthusiasm and interest in the preparation of this book, sending me packages of recollections and photographs. It would almost need a separate reference book to list and thank them individually (likewise the relief agencies – there were nearly 100 in Ethiopia alone). I hope they all will accept acknowledgements for their valued contributions within their own military or civil groups. In spite of extensive research and help I am sure that there are still some who contributed aviation skills in remote areas and who have inevitably been left out – probably so because they were the 'doers' who quietly got on with the job, generating little comment. My own very special thanks must go to the RAF for flying me round Ethiopia to see all aspects of Operation Bushel at first hand, and for granting me the privilege of telling their story.

In the midst of this great endeavour inevitably it is the small, everyday acts of kindness that remain with me – the Operations Officer's few gentle words and proferred cup of tea to a woman, wizened beyond her years by starvation and sickness, waiting in the shade of the aircraft to be transported to hospital – airmovers and loadmasters comforting two tearful chidren, orphaned by famine and torn away from everything familiar, to be flown to a city orphanage – the pilot who, having just delivered an enormous load of food, produced packets of sweets from his flying-suit pockets for airstrip families – the old Ethiopian man living in a hard, bare world who pulled his little donkey's head into his tattered blanket to shield her from the burning sun.

The continual conflict overshadowed the fact that, with international aid and approval, much was done by Ethiopia itself to counter the shortages of the region. But the lessons of the overwhelming value of aviation relief in a hard, cruel world were learned during the famine of 1984-5. I hope this book goes a small way to keeping the world awake to Africa and to highlighting the necessity of speed and efficient logistics when such great tragedies occur. For without them much of the money, the enormous amounts of bulk food and the compassion could have been in vain. A bushel of grain on the quayside at Assab was no consolation to a starving family in the drought-dead Central Ethiopian Highlands. I am sure that the aviators of the world who put their shoulders to the load so valiantly would want to be remembered with just this message.

(opposite page)

Compassion. Flt Lt Phil Jones, 30 Squadron co-pilot and one of the early 'Ops' Officers on Operation Bushel, hands a cup of tea to an old sick woman. Photo John Upsall RAF

Tally board beside the British Military Detachment headquarters – adjusted daily. Photo author

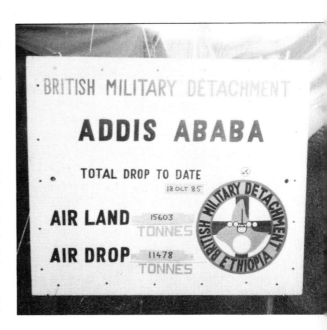

CHAPTER ONE

'Deacon Tango calling Ascot...'

THE radar altimeter beamed off the craggy summits and gulches of the Ethiopian highlands, whipping from 100 feet to 4,000 feet above *terra firma* – to settle finally at 50 feet as the Royal Air Force crew of C-130 Mk 1 Hercules XV178 made a low-level recce over the sudden flatness of the DZ (dropping zone), the wild grass below billowing madly in its wake. The pressure altimeter had shown a descent of just fifty feet to an altitude of 8,825 feet on the QNH.

For this was Derek Amba, a small windswept sun-baked air-drop plateau deep in the wilderness 8,775 feet above sea level which had not been used since before the short season of rain in the spring. Then the crews had been warned to wear flak jackets as protection against rebel interference. And one or two local leaders who carried AK-47 rifles as part of their every-day equipment (a sort of status symbol) had shown excessive zeal, though not necessarily aiming at the aircraft.

Now the only real hazard was the enormous, majestic buzzard which considered itself lord of the skies and, if on a collision course, expected the aircraft to take avoiding action. As the captain, Flight Lieutenant John Clements, an air-drop veteran on his second tour in Ethiopia, and his co-pilot Flight Lieutenant Doug Maugham, both vastly experienced 'truckie' pilots from LXX Squadron, had a long and considered look, everything seemed peaceful below. There was the 47 Air Despatch Squadron safety officer, the smoke from his wind indicator flaring across the drop zone in a frisky 90° crosswind of 15 knots, gusting 25, from the east, his call sign 'Deacon Tango' loud and clear from his little HF PRC 344 radio and acknowledged: "Ascot... ten minutes to drop", by the co-pilot. But for the presence of the Polish Relief Squadron's helicopter and the distinctly portly drab appearance of the 'angel of mercy' food dropping Hercules, it could have been a Biblical scene, with scores and scores of people sitting patiently on the hillside.

The aircraft, one of the 'oldies' of the fleet and the second C-130 to leave Lockheed's Marietta works to join the RAF in 1970, had been tried and trusted in many spheres, not least in 1982 when, after having air refuelling equipment fitted, it established a Hercules endurance record of twenty-eight hours four minutes on a flight

between Ascension Island and the Falklands. Now, in October 1985, it was by no means its first fortnight of hard graft in the thin pure air of the East African mountains. Among its documents was a tattered, roughly drawn chart of the dropping zone by a Herky recce pilot long since returned to the UK. It showed the DZ's 1,500 feet usable length and magnetic heading of 180°, the position and height of the little jutting summits and hills and villages, some of them 100 feet above the DZ, and the tilled areas where the people had endeavoured to grow their own food. It would be handed on to succeeding crews when the present crew's three weeks on Operation Bushel were over – and eventually become someone's memento.

A left-hand circuit and long downwind leg gave plenty of time on the approach to settle the speed at 125 knots with sixty per cent of flap, levelling at forty feet with allowance for drift before passing the threshold. The aim was, in the pushy crosswind, to drop early and slightly to the left of the 'target' from thirty feet or below, low enough to allow each clustered sack of corn to rotate once and land on its pallet.

But inside the aircraft all had been 'action stations' since Doug Maugham had called: "Ten minutes to live drop". At five minutes the two altimeters were compared and checked, the undercarriage locked down (in case of involuntary touch down and to provide drag) the aircraft depressurised and, as the ramp and door were opened by Air Loadmaster Keith Jones, an almost imperceptible wallow synchronous with the 'door open' light on the flight deck. In the hold the four air despatchers, young soldiers of 47 Air Despatch Squadron, a section of the Royal Corps of Transport, who had been lying, relaxed and prone, on top of the cargo, were instantly on their feet. They fitted their 'monkey lines' (safety harness), helmets and gloves ready for the next signal to 'prepare the load', releasing the lashings which restrained the first four tonnes of the sixteen tonnes load. There would be four runs over the DZ, each run dropping four pallets supporting four clusters of loosely packed firmly tied polypropylene sacks of grain.

With two minutes to 'go' and: "Clear live drop" received from the safety officer on the ground the despatch

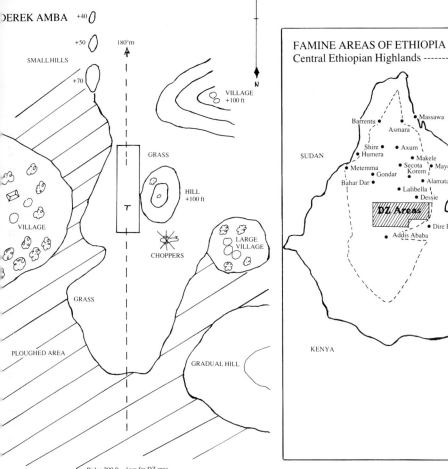

+50

180°m

SMALL HILLS

+70

VILLAGE
+100 ft

GRASS

HILL
+100 ft

VILLAGE

T

LARGE
VILLAGE

CHOPPERS

GRASS

PLOUGHED AREA

GRADUAL HILL

Ridge 200 ft 1nm fm DZ area

FAMINE AREAS OF ETHIOPIA
Central Ethiopian Highlands -------

Barrentu • • Massawa
Asmara

SUDAN

Shire • • Axum
Humera

Makele

Metemma • • Secota • Maychew
• Gondar Korem • Assab

Bahar Dar • • Alamata

• Lalibella
• Dessie DJIBOUTI

DZ Areas

• Dire Dawa

• Addis Ababa

KENYA

SOMALIA

Map of the Derek Amba DZ drawn for air-drop crews by a detachment survey pilot.

crew leader, Corporal Kevin Jones and his team made final preparations. At thirty seconds the loadmaster signalled the despatch crew to remove the chocks for the first drop. The navigator, Flight Lieutenant Doug Marsh, gave a fifteen seconds call and, in the hold, the despatch crew got into final position. The red lights in the hold and flight deck were on and the captain acknowledged Keith's request for a nose high attitude, to abet the laws of gravity. Kevin raised his hand (a back-up in case of lights failure) bringing it down in a chopping motion as the green light flashed on – the signal to cut the final restraints. A push from the despatchers and the two pallets left the aircraft, to be immediately followed by two more. The Hercules nodded gently as, at the controls, the captain felt the trim change. Two seconds after 'green' the engines roared as he climbed out gently to fifty feet. On the descent and on impact most of the sacks left the pallets which broke up –

pallets and sacks and fragments tearing after the aeroplane in a wild fandango of jostle and roll as if begging to be taken aboard again, caught in the void of the big aircraft and an eye-opening example of what can happen to a solid body in the wake of momentum. And though, up front, the Indicated Air Speed was 125 knots, with WAT (weight, altitude and temperature) all high the True Air Speed, as the Hercules delivered, was nearer 140 knots, hence the need for the tough Lancashire-made sacks. Inside the Hercules, in spite of all the skill and experience of every man involved, there had probably been more adrenalin humanly manufactured during those last few seconds of the first drop of the day than that produced during the rest of the day's free dropping.

With the remaining cargo aft in the hold and a temporary forward Centre of Gravity there was trim to readjust for a lighter payload and flaps to reselect at fifty per cent – the normal take-off setting. Now, with less cargo, the threshold speed could be reduced to just over 120 knots. On the second run those gleaming white sacks despatched on the first drop could be plainly seen dead on

First drop of the day at Derek Amba.
Photo author

The final push. Air depatchers of 47 Air Despatch Squadron send two pallets on their way.
Photo author

'target'. And so it was with the second and third live drops until the last four tonnes were blocked by jamming, which can easily happen when a corner gets caught on the side of the aircraft because of turbulence or the load being pushed unevenly. Always on the alert for emergency procedures, the despatch crew manhandled it in seconds to a free position and it was dropped higher up the DZ. They were well aware of the pre-positioned chains and roller chocks which could be quickly placed aft of the load should they need more time to free it, and also the assistance of the pilot who, by flying the aircraft nose down or nose high, 'tilted' the hold and controlled the load's mobility. It had been known, in a bad jam, for the sacks to be thrown out one by one.

The Hercules was to make three more 106 nautical miles flights from its base at Bole Airport, Addis Ababa, each twenty-minute flight carrying sixteen tonnes of grain for the DZ. On the return flight it would pass one of two Transall C-160s of the West German Luftwaffe's Air Transport Wing LTG.61 and 63 which were also air-dropping at Derek Amba. Most of the grain, contributed by worldwide relief agencies, had been transported by rail from the Red Sea ports of Assab and Djibouti to Addis warehouses. Trucked to Bole, it was rebagged into the strong white air-drop sacks on the field by local workers who laboured tirelessly to keep turn-round time to a minimum, sometimes running to the assembly point with two or more sacks on their backs or heads. Here the sacks were weighed and clustered, covered with 'heatshrink' polythene, tied on the pallets and loaded under despatchers' supervision.

Just north of the capital it was difficult to believe that less than ten miles away there had been creeping famine, that the green country below on the outbound flight to Derek Amba had been dead and arid. Now it was a magic, fertile land, a colourful patchwork of crops, teff (the staple diet), maize, sorghum and sesame. The people and their small herds, tranquil in the little treelined villages with their pretty thatched tokuls, went about their daily toil just a few feet below the VFR flight. But the scene soon changed to a dramatic wilderness of barren heights and plunging valleys and river beds which had become dried-up gullies during the past few years – an impassable world from the ground, with the occasional pitiful evidence of terracing by a tiny community endeavouring to grow its own food. The crew identified a rugged escarpment, a landmark in line with the drop zone. Nearer the DZ, an upland area normally capable of feeding its population, it was plain to see that the rains had come and gone and though one crop had been harvested the hoped-for second crop was not expected to reach maturity. A small patch of wild barley, germinated from hardy foreign corn which had spilt from the sacks, had escaped the gleaners' fingers and been blown on to the western slope of the hillside beside the DZ. Its meagre heads would be harvested with care. So the RAF and the Luftwaffe were dropping grain again at Derek Amba, for storage at the request of the Ethiopian Provisional Military Government's Relief and Rehabilitation Commission, before pulling out.

When the mercy flights first free dropped on this DZ earlier in the year they delivered vitally needed food to starving and desperate people. Now Operation Bushel was nearing its end and the final flights to this and other DZs were insurance against an expected re-emergence of food shortage.

But the two western air forces were not the only collaborators on the air dropping mission. At sunrise a Soviet built Mi1 Mi-8 Hip helicopter, one of Russia's largest single rotor helicopters, operated by a crew of the Polish Relief Helicopter Squadron, left Lidetta, Addis Ababa's military airfield, whenever and wherever an air-drop was planned. With its three man crew of captain, co-pilot and engineer it carried the British drop zone safety officer, his assistant and their equipment. En route to Derek Amba there was generally a call at Calala, a small but busy upcountry settlement with two hospitals run by European health agencies, where up to thirty-six sacks of Russian grain was delivered and there was an interchange of passengers, mostly health and relief workers. This 'milk run' was obviously the big event of the day at Calala. The friendly crews of this highly efficient and useful aircraft built up a tremendous rapport with their Air Despatch Squadron passengers, providing food and drink for the long day ahead on the DZ and sometimes supplying equipment, such as Very-pistol and flame gun as well. Captain Antonio Tusiehics, his co-pilot Lieutenant Adam Choltiy and engineer Lieutenant Antony Myslinski flew the back-up helicopter for free drop from Hercules XV178. Their rapprochement with Peter Eginton, the despatch safety officer, and his assistant, Jock Redpath, was a mixture of very basic English, sign language, enthusiasm and laughter that was both efficient and effective.

Already, as the helicopter arrived at Derek Amba the village elders were clearing the drop zone of masses of people and their animals, using switches indiscriminately but without malice. Peter's first task was to set up the

Safety officer Sgt Peter Eginton and his assistant,
Driver Jock Redpath set up the bright yellow
markers on the threshold of the DZ.
Photo author

Old and young and their animals wait patiently in the early morning sun for an air-drop at Derek Amba. Photo author

Harvest Home. Carrying the corn to the village store. Photo author

radio and test it, establish the bright yellow plastic markers on the DZ (which frequently ended the day shredded to bits by a low flying Transall under-carriage, running in at fifteen feet) and then, as the dot in the southerly sky identified itself as XV178's first flight of the day, scare the birds and final stragglers with the Very-pistol, indicate wind direction and velocity with a smoke flare and call the Hercules in. After completing its first four drops it was soon followed by the first of the two Luftwaffe Transalls, both called in by Peter.

The people waited patiently on the hillside in the bright early morning sun as the first two food dropping aircraft followed each other, each leaving its donation of dazzling white sacks in the grass. It was all a question of timing and, with forty minutes loading time between the first and second Transalls, the villagers descended like locusts on the DZ to hump the unbroken bags (a successful major-

Loading small Ethiopian asses with grain sacks to carry to the village store. Photo author

ity) to an assembly point. Here, as the mountain of grain bags grew and were tallied by a RRC official, the pretty little Ethiopian asses arrived with their drovers to be loaded with sacks to convey them to the village store. Those who had no donkey carried them manually up the long hillside, two sacks at a time for adults, one for children. For it was very much a family affair, with generations and their animals, goats, sheep and donkeys spending the day by the zone. The very old took care of the very young – bundled in blankets on the lea of the hillside against the hot-cold blow of the wind while the able-bodied got on with the job.

The collection of grain was highly organised. An elder directed operations with a megaphone, under supervision from an official of the RRC who was in charge of the village warehouse where the grain would be stored. One or two people wandered around importantly, each armed with a Soviet rifle. It was all rather bossy – in the manner of Marxist regimes. Then, when all the sacks were carried away from the DZ to the assembly point, the gleaners were allowed to descend on the dropping zone, children and the elderly who gathered the torn sacks and the spilt grain, harvesting each precious seed of corn by hand until cleared for the next wave of air dropping. And so it went on, all day.

It was all in anticipation of an expected food shortage, if not famine, in this remote, primitive and beautiful

corner of Africa. When Operation Bushel became just a memory and the time arrived for another scramble for survival the people would queue with their traditional dignity and patience beside the storehouse. The Ethiopian Government's area superviser would issue each one with 500 grams a day, a bare subsistence allowance. Now as XV178's last drop of the day was completed and, overhead the DZ, it set course for Addis, the four despatchers sat on the open ramp, their legs hanging over the edge, with nothing between them and the ground but the hard ramp and their monkey lines. They waved 'goodnight' to the people below and, in lengthening shadows, the Hercules disappeared over the southern horizon. Peter and Jock were retrieving the plastic shreds of their yellow markers and packing up the radio, flare gun and Very-pistol. As they trudged back to the helicopter with their equipment, the crew were loading bundles of reusable sacks, emptied and returned from the village storehouse. By the time they arrived back in Lidetta the short tropic dusk was fading, the end of another long day by the dropping zone.

Crew of the Polish Relief Helicopter Squadron at Derek Amba. (from left): co-pilot, Lt Adam Chottiy; engineer, Lt Antony Myslinski; captain, Cpt Antonio Tusiehics. Photo author

Humping the unbroken sacks from DZ to assembly point. Photo author

CHAPTER TWO

Flying on Thin Air

ALL internal flying over Ethiopia was under Visual Flight Rules (VFR). Ground based navigation aids were almost non-existent and those at the few airfields such as Assab and Asmara often inaccurate and subject to interference from thunderstorms. While the Hercules is fitted with excellent Omega navigation and doppler systems the crews preferred Mark 1 eyeball all the way, over such remote and distinctive terrain, using the doppler to correct drift. Occasions when systems went on the blink were rare – but it could happen. Knowing position at all times by the visual use of landmarks, dry salt lakes, river beds, mountain ranges, escarpments and the odd shapes of summits or gullies was basic but effective. Each succeeding crew was familiarised with terrain eccentricities. Because of the almost continuous heat haze by day and chill mists at sunrise and sundown most of the flights were below 10,000 feet (amsl), mountain-hopping 'Grand Canyon' style flying, coping with low level mid-morning turbulence as the heat of the sun beckoned the rising air. Standing waves over the wild, awe inspiring country with sudden changes of ground level from a few feet below to an abyss of 4,000 feet or more in depth, could cause a heavy aircraft, suddenly hitting the bottomless air-pocket, to drop like a stone.

Even 'low' flying was at altitudes where the average Westerner can start showing early symptoms of hypoxia or lack of oxygen. At 10,000 feet only two-thirds as much oxygen is taken in with each breath as at sea level. Apart from the Red Sea areas all the tactical flying was at these heights and the aircraft had to be depressurised before the door was opened for air dropping. It could frequently be open for up to thirty minutes.

Fit people have few problems flying on thin air up to 12,500 feet and are less affected than those who smoke, drink excessively or are unhealthy. But it was recognised that tactical exercises such as air dropping in these conditions required top performance at all times and stringent military rules on supplementary oxygen use were applied.

The radar altimeter, the most relevant and most monitored of all aircraft instruments over Ethiopia, was constantly checked with the pressure altimeter for its accuracy and warning automation above such inhospitable terrain, often just a few feet below, were vital to safety.

Aircrew members of the four Hercules squadrons, old hands of the Falklands campaign, found similarities, not least in the dearth of communications, so different from the voluble clatter and chatter in more populated areas such as Europe. Here there were two choices – the simple but very efficient Ethiopian HF radio on frequency 5536 or the approach and tower frequencies of Addis, Asmara or Assab. These could be used as a blind call when out of range, keeping contact with the second airborne Hercules and other relief flights, and letting them know position and intentions.

Disabling bird strikes were the major airborne hazard. The bane of most airfields the world over, birds like grain and they naturally congregated at distribution centres, dropping zones and airstrips where grain was loaded, unloaded and often spilt. Years of drought have made vultures, buzzards and numerous smaller breeds which live in flocks both cunning and doughty. At Bole the pigeons got so bloated they could barely fly, waddling and flapping across the runway before the aircraft. However, the local birds of prey kept them within manageable proportions, availing themselves of a glut of plump, overfed pigeon. Across country the magnificent, ferocious African buzzard had territorial rights with fear of no-one and nothing, least of all direct confrontation with a marauding Fat Albert which it considered a rival. Bevies of smaller birds tended to follow their leader in blind Kamikaze formation. Corrective or evasive actions were extremely difficult in a heavily laden aircraft flying at drop speed below thirty-five feet. Up to three birdstrikes a week were not uncommon and engineers became familiar with the gruesome task of fishing out gory feathers and bits of heads, flesh and beaks from a holed wing or fuselage – while contemplating the dire results. More than one wing leading edge was extensively damaged by large birds, grounding aircraft until spare parts could be flown out from Lyneham in the resupply Hercules.

One of the first of such mid-air collisions happened in December 1984 just a few weeks after arrival at Addis, when an enormous maribu stork flew straight into the wing. There was a resounding bang as it was ingested inboard of No. 3 engine, late in the afternoon on a homebound flight from Makalle, one of the major distribution

centres, to Addis. It bent the control rods on the side of the wing and gave the captain, Squadron Leader Jeff Bullen, and his crew some unhappy moments. When they transported the bird back to base there were some ribald remarks about bringing home the Christmas dinner – the conclusion being that it was far too ugly! On a later occasion a fifteen-pound vulture entered the aircraft below the cockpit, taking out the radome on the nose. This necessitated a limp home, looking decidedly down in the mouth, to Marshall of Cambridge, sustainers-in-chief of the Hercules fleet, for extensive repairs.

Another captain, Flight Lieutenant Ray Bond of LXX Squadron vividly remembers his own experience on April 27th 1985.

"It was the first drop of the morning at Rabel. We had arrived early and the DZ party was not yet there. We flew around and completed our air-dropping checks. We noticed, at the time, that there were some large flocks of birds about."

In the hold the loadmaster was monitoring the final preparation for despatch. On the flightdeck a large flock of pigeon-sized birds could be seen, a black mass looming up. With the aircraft less than fifty feet above ground at low airspeed, they could not have arrived at a worse moment. The impact came just as the loadmaster called: "Load moving."

"We could hear them hitting the starboard wing. The No 4 engine rpms dropped to eighty-five per cent and the turbine temperature started to rise rapidly, followed by a violent yawing, left and right. My co-pilot, Mick Crossey reported flames coming out of the engine's jet piping."

He added with typical aircrew understatement: "It had no further use so we shut it down and climbed away very gently on three. But with the first four tonnes gone we were nose heavy – well outside the normal trim. Fortunately the ground below was downhill, though there was sharply rising ground ahead. With 26,000 pounds of grain down the back, the loadmaster had to close the doors and reposition it before we could fly back and land at Addis".

Such a contingency was frequently practised on training sessions in the simulator, and the crew calmly carried out the emergency drill and 'lost engine' checks and kept cool heads. Needless to say both engine and propeller needed replacing.

"It's afterwards that you stop and think what might have happened", Ray added.

Later, he was awarded a 'Green Endorsement' – a treasured certificate in his logbook – for his airmanship and the exemplary way he had handled the crisis.

But apart from reluctant confrontation with the local feathered fraternity, the Hercules squadrons found the

Mountain hopping VFR flying to Assab. Hercules captain Flt Lt Chris Kingswood of 47 Squadron at the controls. Photo author

From the Hercules flight deck. A pretty little Ethiopian village north of Addis Ababa. Photo author

flying an exhilarating challenge. The operation's training value was immediately acknowledged by all, from those in the MoD to every instructor, pilot and crew, air mover and despatcher, and if it was an expensive way of acquiring a unique and unrepeatable experience, it was at least a very satisfying one. "Doing a real job", as so many of them put it, was a significant part of the challenge.

Because the climate and flying conditions were both gruelling and exacting, all aircrew returned home after a three-weeks stint. In theory the work roster was one day on, one day off, a working day consisting of twelve hours duration or more. In practice many, many gave up their free days to muck in, if there were sickness or engineering problems, to keep the aircraft flying. Arriving at Addis to find themselves immediately ushered into the detachment commander's briefing, at the crack of dawn the next morning they were in a minibus or car heading for the airport to work or fly with an established crew, from whom they would take over. Aircrew would fly, air-landing or air-dropping, with their predecessors on a very revealing sit-in to remote airstrips or DZs, the captain and crew of the flight giving them the benefit of their own previous three-weeks experience operating in conditions where WAT were more than significant.

As with the drop zones, the early survey pilots on landing sorties sketched their own approach and landing charts for each airstrip. A complete set of pilot drawn landing charts of all the strips in use was included among the aircraft documents during its air land detachment. If there was a diversion or sudden change of plans the 'Nav-strips' were all there. They showed the length, width and direction of the runways, the position of normal hazards and some cryptic clues such as 'shitehawks' or 'Boris', indicating the presence of buzzards or Russian hardware! The altitude of each strip, WAT limits and maximum take-off and landing weights were recorded underneath with spaces for filling in the current payload and temperature, safety altitude, fuel reserves and communications (if any).

By far the most taxing exercise that the Hercules has been required to perform was the continual landing on these harsh, hot and high airstrips serving the inland Ethiopian townships and distribution stations. Seven or eight landings a day wreaked havoc in these conditions and each aircraft on air land operations was savaged, necessitating a far shorter turn-round time than that for people. Tyres, undercarriage and piping suffered frequent damage and abrasions, scores and pits – even holes in the underbelly – were common. With the addition of birdstrike damage there was an enormous repair bill, each aircraft limping home to Lyneham for a spell in the hangar or for major repairs to Marshall of Cambridge.

At first tyres, cut and ruined, many of them shredded to their fibrous interior, had to be changed nearly every day. One crew was thrown in at the deep end during the first few days of operation when XV187, captained by Flight Lieutenant Paul Spears, blew one of its four main wheel tyres on runway rocks at Axum, seriously damaging equipment in undercarriage housing. Paul had been delivering grain all day at Makalle and his lift to Axum where the other aircraft, XV186, captained by Flight Lieutenant Tony Evans had been landing, was the last scheduled flight of the day.

"It was sitting on the ground as we rolled past it. There was the usual lot of noise and I was aware we were not slowing down as fast as we should. Tony's co-pilot told us we had burst a tyre. I pulled off the runway but couldn't feel any handling problems. However, when we got out it was obvious it was in one heck of a state," Paul recalled.

Huge chunks of rubber had stripped off the tyre and flailed into the starboard undercarriage. They were faced with the need to get the wheel off but were not carrying bulky tyres and jacks, to make maximum weight available for grain. It was too late for the other aircraft to return to Addis and fly up with spares.

At first there appeared to be two choices – to somehow fly home or to stay overnight. The crew were offered accommodation in the town but this was politely declined. If

Removing a wing leading edge on XV209 after a bird strike. Photo Geoff Whyham RAF

Damage to leading edge, condenser and anti-icing wiring after Hercules XV178/buzzard mid-air. Photo author (inset)

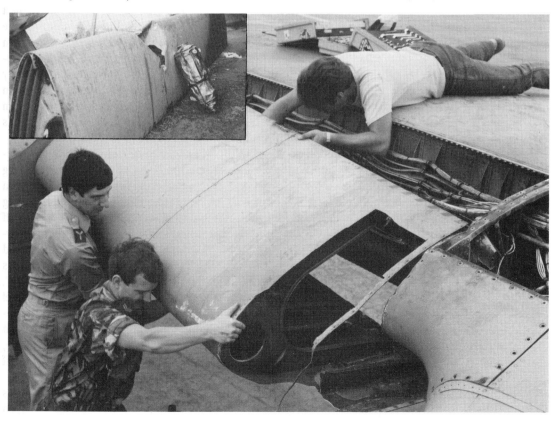

immobilised in the field, they would stay with their aircraft and were equipped with 'go-packs' of rations, sleeping bags and survival gear, normally carried for forced landing exigencies. But choice was eliminated when the Ethiopian defence force commander came aboard and advised them that there was a battle raging north of Axum and that if things went badly for them the airfield could be surrounded and captured. Everything of value, including the aircraft, would be blown up. There was a marked feeling of get-home-itis.

The day was saved by the flight engineer. Before he left Lyneham, Flight Sergeant Steve Ponting collected all documents, ancient and modern, which could be useful in terrain or war situations, among them a couple of sheets of instructions on battle damage repairs in the Vietnam war – a combat-get-you-home advisory method of removing the wheel without jacks.

The Hercules undercarriage drops vertically, unlike the lateral system of most heavy aircraft, and the wheel has to be physically lifted off the ground. Steve and his willing helpers followed the instructions on the tatty bits of paper, unhinging the tensioners (load restraints) from the aircraft hold, winding them round the oleo and, with the leverage of a large piece of piping found by the navigator, twisting and twisting until it was raised from the ground. They bent the piping at right angles, upsetting the brigade commander who had been waiting for his water pipe for the last three months.

Steve chained up the damaged axle and oleo and as darkness fell Paul took off on 'three wheels' and flew back to Addis wheels down. They approached Addis to find themselves in the midst of arriving Russian An-12s, and it was decreed by Air Traffic Control that XV187 should land last because of its dicey landing gear.

"The take-off and flight home had been uneventful. Now we hung around, with fuel getting low and no-where else to go. Then one Russian went off the end and almost blocked the runway", said Paul.

A quick decision had to be made. Nearly out of fuel, he elected to land over the top of the wreck on what limited runway was left – on his three remaining mainwheels. It was a permitted manoeuvre but one which needed some degree of flying skill. It had been quite a day.

In the 1986 New Year Honours List, Paul, one of the first and also the last pilot to take the final flight on Operation Bushel out of Ethiopia, was awarded the Queen's Commendation for Valuable Services in the Air. Steve was awarded an Air Officer Commanding-in-Chief's Commendation for his engineering prowess which made the unconventional take-off and landing possible.

It became clear that, whatever the damage, it was imperative to fly the aircraft out of the strips before nightfall if humanly and mechanically possible because of the risk of rebel activity. Staying out at night could cause all sorts of predicaments, perhaps even culminating in fatalities, if not the capture or disablement of an aircraft. For a Hercules represented untold booty to a band of marauding guerrillas on nocturnal foray. Apart from the fact that the aircraft was needed the following day, another limiting factor was a curfew at Addis. Captains were instructed to be airborne after the last delivery of the day and on course for base at least one hour before dusk. This limited the flights of each aircraft to three a day. If there were mechanical problems on an airstrip there were two choices – advice and briefing to the ground engineer and aircrew over the HF radio or a diversion of the second Hercules with engineers and spares. An overnight stop at Makalle was narrowly avoided by borrowing spares from a Transamerica L-100-30 Hercules delivering grain for the International Red Cross. Although it is sods law that aeroplanes go on sick parade at the least opportune moment, it says much for the aircraft itself and its attendants that no Hercules on Operation Bushel spent a night in hostile territory. Like wounded homing pigeons, they limped back to the loft.

Quite apart from the degradations of aircraft perfor-

Lift-off on the dirt strip at Makalle for a return flight to Assab to pick up a second load of grain.
Photo author

mance brought about by the altitude, before the rainy season started dust and sandstorms in areas of extreme drought caused other problems. Sandstorms could bring visibility down to nil, and dust ingestion could wreak havoc on engines and piping. The dreaded haboob, nature's most vicious phenomenon, could appear out of no-where, its dust devils dancing a fiendish fandango in gale force winds and gigantic all-enveloping clouds of sand up to 7,000 feet high. A sudden sombre sky, and there it was. Camels closed their nostrils, other beasts turned their backs and shut their eyes, humans pulled their robes and blankets over their heads. Aircraft could only be turned downwind, with all vents and apertures closed. Light aircraft could be mauled into heaps of rubble. The only use for desert dust was that the movement of any vehicle or herd near the airstrip determined wind direction from miles away – and drift could be set by the movement of the red cloud of dust after take-off!

For the pilots every strip was a new experience, and 'getting in', with WAT critical, was akin to coaxing a living creature. Each landing was a tactical 'gumshield' arrival dispensing with the luxury of a flare – firmly, gently with the immediate application of brakes and reverse thrust on touchdown to shorten a ride of the Valkyries over rocks and stones – reminding the crew all too well what was happening below as they listened to the mad tattoo on the underbelly. Land too fast (with the disproportion between IAS and TAS) and the speed could be above that at which the nosewheel could cope and tyres would disintegrate. Trim was vital. The pilots had enough to concentrate the mind without the added interest of an aeroplane that was nose- or tail-heavy. Finding the strip in the first place, with no air traffic control assistance, determining a threshold often buried in vegetation, avoiding animals (a take-off had to be aborted at one strip because of a wandering camel, a go-around had to be initiated to avoid air-dropping on an old man on a donkey trotting across a DZ), and looking out for rebel movements were quite enough to contend with. One short airstrip necessitated negotiating a fifteen-degree bend during take-off and landing to avoid mountains, trees and a village.

Similar manoeuvres were sometimes needed to avoid sharpshooters. The situation could change from day to day with guerillas descending on airstrips and then trooping away to the hills as government troops took control. The world heard very little about a war that was far more extensive than the Government would admit, but there was often heavy fighting and many casualties. Anxious to avoid an international incident, Ethiopian brigade

Racing its stocky shadow over moonlike salt basins near the Red Sea. Photo author

commanders would keep the RAF posted as to the latest situation near the trouble spots.

It was ironic that the Government had actually come to power in a military coup after student riots against the previous Government's handling of a famine. It was sometimes difficult to comprehend who was fighting whom. Ethiopian history has been dominated by a hopeless struggle to unify eight major national groups, and by its crucial position in the Horn of Africa. Though now there was an uneasy peace in the Ogaden, there was a fifteen years unending war over the annexation of Eritrea. The Eritreans themselves could not agree on what they wanted and their liberating forces were split into three factions, the Popular Liberation Forces, the Eritrea Liberation Front and the Eritrean Liberation Forces. Any one of them could be threatening the Red Sea ports, Asmara or Axum. In Tigre the unrest was more recent, caused by a demand since 1975 for 'home rule' by the Tigre Popular Liberation Forces. Less organised than the Eritrean forces, they were known to descend in bands and kidnap aid workers or anyone foolish enough to be touring – all of them released unharmed.

To contain so much unrest the Ethiopian Army of 306,000 troops was the largest in black Africa. It represented forty-six per cent of the country's annual budget and the nation was said to be in debt to Russia by three billion dollars. Upcountry Red Cross charter pilots talked unhappily of an Ethiopian MiG-23 shot down by a rebel missile. It was a hazardous situation for neutral flyers of vulnerable aeroplanes.

Raising the dust prior to take-off at Alamata, a remote Wollo province airstrip.
Photo Geoff Whyham RAF

Assab, the major forward operating base, was also WAT critical, but with differences. At forty-six feet above sea level in sweltering, dusty heat and a frequent crosswind of forty-five knots, the aircraft was required to lift-off with a cargo of grain often in excess of 40,000 pounds. As the crews were warned when they first arrived – "pull it off and it won't want to come. It's a hot envelope for this aircraft."

The flight from Addis to Assab was 335 miles and about one hour thirty minutes flying time. Thereafter, most flights loaded with grain for the airstrips were of about one hour's duration. The outbound flight from Addis to Assab was a potted tour of the country in itself, with all the spectacular changes of scenery that are typical of Ethiopia. Just north of the capital was the first area to recover after the drought broke, a fertile area full of the pretty little African villages, treelined farms, crops and herds – soon to change into a sparsely populated mountain world of tiny terraced settlements clinging to one wild, inhospitable escarpment after another. The mountains then suddenly gave way to a lowland desert waste as the Hercules raced its stocky shadow over moonlike salt basins, white as hoar frost, as it neared the Red Sea.

Rather than rely on Assab's prima donna NDB the crews preferred to navigate by an easily recognised coastal promontory to line up with Runway 13, a down-sloping unmade hard compacted gravel and earth airstrip of 11,000 feet. However, with an indeterminate end, only its first 6,000 feet were decreed usable. North of the sea port, it had the appearance of the last airfield on earth, surrounded by salt levels and, after the high, pure inland air, as if the sun had pinpointed that one spot on which to blaze. However, it did possess one large maintenance hangar, a road from the port and a control tower, and there were rudimentary flight information and weather reporting facilities. Marshalling was indifferent and many a Herc had to reverse-thrust itself out of a rut before taking on cargo.

It soon became clear that there was little chance of RAF military aircraft being permitted to deliver food in the rebel-held far north of Tigre province or Eritrea where some of the worst drought areas were situated. The RAF could only deliver in Government-held areas and declare itself strictly 'neutral'. However, most of the northern towns were in Government hands and many starving refugees had fled from the fighting in the countryside to form huge settlements beside the feeding centres in southern Tigre and northern Wollo such as Makalle, Gondar, Axum and Korem. After January 1985 when the Ethiopians allowed one aircraft to be used for air dropping, the defects bill reduced, though to be fair, local airfield workers and villagers had no small hand in this improvement, for as soon as they understood the needs of aircraft much heavier than their normal callers, mission light aircraft or Ethiopian Airlines DC-3s, they set to work with a will to keep the strips free of stones, flints and impediments.

CHAPTER THREE

Answering the Call of Hunger

THE RAF became involved immediately after the crisis in Africa had dominated the United Nations General Assembly meeting in October 1984. During the last week of the month Air Commodore Bill Croydon, Director of Air Support for the Ministry of Defence, with a wealth of experience as a heavy transport pilot, was summoned to a meeting with Lord Trefgarne, Under Secretary for the Armed Forces, and asked to produce an aid package that the RAF could offer Ethiopia. Already the Transport Wing at Lyneham was champing at the bit, for Oxfam had begged them to move 15,000 tonnes of grain from Assab to the famine areas. Now a decision was urgent as the Ethiopian Commissioner for Relief and Rehabilitation, Major Dawitt Wolde-Giorjis was expected in London at the weekend. After consultation with him it was obvious that the situation was so horrendous that any modest contribution, such as one or two aircraft for one month, as was first suggested, was not enough.

"Our knowledge was scanty but after meeting Dawitt we felt we knew more about the situation. All we knew about the airfields was that there were three, two of them military and the one civil airport, Bole at Addis Ababa, comparatively well equipped", Air Commodore Croydon said.

Timothy Raison, then Minister for Overseas Development Administration, accepted two Hercules to fly through daylight hours on air-land and air-drop duties for an already open-ended three months.

Meanwhile RAF Lyneham, home of the Transport Wing, was gearing up for a rapid deployment to Ethiopia. On Friday October 26th the station commander, Group Captain John Cheshire, called a meeting of squadron commanders to outline a plan to send the Hercules on famine relief. Potentially two aircraft would be sent, the detachment would be self-contained for administration and the primary task would be to transport grain from Port Assab to a number of inland airstrips. Where the aircraft would be based was unclear. The potential dangers in a Marxist country to people and aircraft from a Western military organisation were difficult to assess. There was an obvious security threat at Assab, southern port in the unhappy province of Eritrea, and the northern airfields. It was strongly felt that Addis Ababa was the only practical choice for detachment headquarters.

Previous experience had proved that air-dropping was the most effective way of feeding beleaguered people and early plans included preparation for air-drop by a self-contained detachment of six four-man air despatch crews. Both air-land and air-drop have advantages – basically airlanding is the fastest, cheapest and least resource-intensive method of delivery in a broad area, but it requires an airstrip. Free drop is slower, with a much lighter payload, and requires equipment, special sacks, base-boards and ties (none of them were available in Ethiopia), but is still the most effective way of speedily putting food into the mouths of remote and hungry people. But at that time, it was not to be.

By mid-afternoon on the same day the station was alerted to almost certain deployment. It was a hectic weekend. Operations Wing experts on the performance data of the aircraft set to work to calculate the impact in and out of every known strip in Ethiopia but with few charts and ignorance of the latest conditions these were sketchy. There was considerable confusion as to what to take. However, Transamerica Airlines crews, who had been intermittently operating three L-100-30 Hercules in and out of Assab and the larger strips for the past two months, lifting eighteen tonnes daily to the crisis areas, were consulted to identify which strips were feasible for landing, the basic needs and essential equipment. The United Kingdom Mobile Air Movements Squadron (UKMAMS) based at Lyneham were tasked with packing the necessities in the minimum number of aircraft. Four airstrip qualified crews from the two tactical Squadrons, LXX and No. 47, were on standby. Engineers were preparing the aircraft.

On the following Monday Air Commodore Croydon and Lord Trefgarne met the Prime Minister.

"There were a number of questions to be answered", Bill Croydon said. "Who was to pay for the operation – Defence or the Overseas Development Administration (ODA) for whom we were providing the aircraft – an estimated £1 million a month, with an open-ended commitment? Mrs Thatcher didn't mind – just as long as we got on with it. We were now looking at sending two aircraft which would be entirely self-sufficient, with four crews,

Transamerica Airlines L-100-30 Super Hercules. Their crews were consulted by the RAF before flying in to Bole. Photo Southern Air Transport

either in a dropping or landing capacity".

Having obtained the Prime Minister's go-ahead, it was agreed that costs for the three months operation would be funded from the defence budget. The next hurdle was the green light from Ethiopia. With everyone ready to go, there was much diplomatic to-ing and fro-ing. Some aspects of the plan were unacceptable to the Ethiopians. Relief aircraft were expected from other nationalities and there was an impending Organisation of Arab Unity conference at Addis Ababa. There was panic at the prospect of extra movements and apron overcrowding at Bole. The Ethiopians were wary of what the RAF might get up to and who would get the supplies. And they totally rejected air-dropping as too difficult to control, a view reluctantly supported by the British Embassy.

"Ethiopia did not realise what sort of capabilities we had. They viewed us with a great deal of suspicion – afraid that we might drop food to rebel factions or that they would appropriate it. The next problem was getting visas", Bill Croydon recalled.

That a Marxist regime should actually allow Western military detachments into the country was formerly unheard of and spoke for its desperation. At the time the Italian Embassy was the only Western embassy to be allowed military representation. But agreement was finally reached for air-landing operations, to last three months.

Two squadron leaders from No. 1 Group HQ at Upavon, experts in logistics and tactical transport operations, were the first to be granted visas by the Ethiopian Embassy. They became an advance party from the moment they returned to Whitehall from the embassy at 5.30 pm. They were given a police escort for a twenty-two minutes hair-raising drive through the West End to catch the 6.00 pm Ethiopian Airlines schedule, one of five weekly flights from Heathrow to Addis, the day after the Prime Minister's sanction had been received. John Morley, with many years experience of operating the Hercules in its tactical role and Brian Morgan, an air-movements specialist, became military attachés to the British Embassy in Addis Ababa and were charged with setting up 'Operation Bushel'.

John Morley and Brian Morgan ran into immediate arguments as to where the aircraft should be based. Twenty-six Warsaw Pact 'mercy' aircraft were expected: Soviet, East German and Libyan, as well as two West German Luftwaffe C-160 Transalls. Djibouti, an independent republican state, was suggested and then Assab, both impractical for a number of reasons, not least the constant forty to forty-five knots dust-filled, sweltering crosswinds off the Red Sea and the security and accommodation problems at Assab. Somewhat reluctantly, the Ethiopian Government agreed to the British base at Bole Airport – for a fortnight, until the start of the OAU conference. And there it remained, using Assab as a forward operating base only, to the end of the operation.

The first task for the two officers was to send back a situation report on the day after arrival. This allowed the

Ready for immediate deployment. Some of the RAF's original sixty-two strong fleet of C-130s, Mk1s and Mk 3s, at their home base RAF Lyneham. Photo RAF Lyneham (previous page)

detachment to be finely tuned to immediate necessities. With everyone based at Addis the security problems were re-assessed. Numbers were trimmed to those needed to airlift grain from Assab to inland airstrips at Axum and Makalle.

*   *   *

It had become clear that a race to contribute military aid was developing between Western and Eastern Bloc countries. Lyneham, on standby with a reputation for rapid reaction to any world-wide requirement, was getting decidedly itchy feet. Ethiopian clearance was not yet forthcoming but in a calculated gamble a fleet of seven aircraft was dispatched to Akrotiri on a presumption that agreement would be reached. Permission to land in Ethiopia arrived while they were airborne.

The first three Hercules left Lyneham on Thursday November 1st, to be followed during the next twenty-four hours by four more. Hopeful to the last that air-dropping would be permitted, one carried 47 Air Despatch Squadron crews and equipment, but when it became clear that their skills were unacceptable by Ethiopia, it was turned back at Cyprus, where they had all night-stopped. Bitterly disappointed that its efforts had been spurned, the Army did in fact provide valuable assistance in the preparation stage with full intelligence, health and hygiene briefings for the conditions expected, and also provided a two-man Royal Engineers water purification team from 9 Parachute Squadron to set up a water bowser, and a Royal Corps of Transport signals team from 29 Transport and Movements Regiment to accompany the detachment. Two despatchers also continued, on a fact finding mission. It soon became apparent that there would be plenty to do – even without air-dropping.

They arrived – a 76-strong company – into a world of ochre and brown. The few old hands who had been there before remembered a pure-aired capital surrounded by a fertile and colourful countryside, so fertile in fact that double cropping had been the norm. Now the green acres had crumbled into a parched earth, brought about by four years of drought, a ghost world, the only green that of a drab and pathetic thistle, edible to neither man nor beast. It was a world almost abandoned by its own Government, struggling with ideological wars as well as the cruel twists of nature and finding it all too much. Looking down on the last few hundred miles of flight, it was plain to see a cremated heartland.

Raising the dust! Reverse thrust from one of pioneer Transamerica Airlines' L-100-30s as it lands on an Ethiopian airstrip.
Photo Southern Air Transport

As dawn broke and Bole Airport opened on Saturday November 3rd, airport workers watched as the first rugged RAF Mk 1 Hercules, XV186, in its disruptive patterned camouflage (light aircraft grey/dark sea grey/dark green!) appeared on the skyline, touched down and taxied in. With Sudan and Ethiopia at loggerheads, no military aircraft was permitted to land in Ethiopia if it had overflown Sudan and so over Egypt there had to be some skirting around, using the Red Sea VOR at Jeddah and a southerly track to Addis of 180° on the 360° radial.

For Flight Lieutenant Nigel Watson, captain of the leading Hercules, his co-pilot Flying Officer Steve Drurey, their 47 Squadron crew and advance party passengers there had been very little sleep since they had said goodbye to the green hills of Wiltshire. They had turned in for a very few hours at Akrotiri, to set off at midnight with the full intention of arriving at Bole Airport at first light ready for a full day's work and for the aircraft to enter the operations field before the day was over. On board was Wing Commander Barry Nunn, a senior officer from Upavon with responsibilities for the Hercules tactical role. He was to be the first detachment commander. Also on

board were operations staff, a MAMS team, a doctor, the other 47 Squadron crew captained by Flight Lieutenant Tony Evans and two LXX Squadron crews, skippered by Flight Lieutenants Paul Spears and Terry Locke. They were the pioneer crews of Operation Bushel.

There was the inevitable reception party of Ethiopian Provisional Military Government officials and worthies, the British Embassy and the Press, to whom patience and courtesy must be extended though the aviators were longing to get on with the job of unloading and making the aircraft available for work. But they were touched by the warmheartedness of the welcome, and they had their first meeting with their military adviser, Colonel Escheti, who was to become the tireless linkman between the Ethiopian Government and the detachment, and his aide, Colonel Tsegaye.

The four tactical crews spent the morning listening to survey reports and flight planning, while the others sorted

The airlift gets under way with all the grain and a large local workforce waiting at Assab.
Photo by author

out accommodation. Nigel Watson and his crew prepared the aircraft for a strip recce of the three major landing areas – to determine minimum compliance and suitability as 'Hercules temporary landing zones'. The flight commenced at midday and three strips were visited – Assab, Makalle and Axum. On board was Colonel Tsegaye (who acted as translator and introduced them to airfield authorities), the detachment commander, the two LXX Squadron crews and Squadron Leader Morley, who was charged with surveying all the strips.

"It was clear that the Ethiopians were very keen for us to get on with the job", Nigel Watson recalled. "We had a six-hours sortie, first overflying each airstrip to have a good look and then overshooting two or three times before landing."

At Assab there was no sign of grain and no evidence of lorries and, when they landed, apparently no arrangements for moving grain from the port to the airport, except when Red Cross-Transamerica flights were expected. Wing Commander Nunn and Col Tsegaye went down to the port and were assured that the grain would be moved to the airport.

At each airfield they stayed as briefly as possible on the ground, keeping the engines running. As Nigel made a couple of approaches into Axum the colonel became decidedly twitchy, emphasising that the southerly hills abounded with rebels and that a one-way approach, turning in front of a distinctive sugar-loaf rock to the north, was the only safe way in. But by and large they returned to Addis reasonably optimistic about the task ahead.

"The strips were better than we expected and runways longer than they were charted. A lot of my fears were allayed. We flew back happy – provided the grain was delivered to the aircraft", said Paul Spears, one of the LXX Squadron skippers.

They climbed wearily out of the Hercules into the darkness of the airport pan, a bunch of very tired flyers. It had seemed a long, long time since breakfast at Akrotiri.

While the recce flight was in progress the two other Hercules which had left Lyneham on the Thursday arrived at Addis, the first of these a 30 Squadron Mk 3 'stretched' Hercules, XV219. Both aircraft bulged with 'kit' – engineering stores, movements equipment, field kitchens, tents, medical stores (for both detachment use and onward transportation) and all the small, urgent requirements stuffed in every odd corner and swamping the Ethiopian Airlines maintenance ramp as they were speedily unloaded. So base camp was struck! – established by people and equipment arriving on the first three aircraft.

It consisted of two tents in a corner of the airport pan – one an operations centre and the other a general assembly-cum-tea-room-cum-get-out-of-the-sun refuge – and there they remained, headquarters of the British Military Detachment, during its fourteen months sojourn in Ethiopia.

Operations proper commenced the next day, on Sunday November 4th, when XV186 carried its first load of grain for famine relief from Assab to Makalle, captained by Tony Evans with a 47 Squadron Special Forces Flight crew and a team of airmovers. At Assab they were delighted to find all the grain they could lift waiting at the airfield with a large local workforce. As the airlift got under way three more C-130s which had left Lyneham on November 2nd were flying into Addis loaded with heavy equipment, a Land Rover, a power unit, water and rations and the very necessary water filtration and purification plant. Captain of one of the supply aircraft was Squadron Leader Mike Bradstock-Smith, a performance specialist from the Support Training Squadron.

"We knew that operating at high altitudes, the high weights and ambient temperatures of the region would test the aircraft to the limits of its performance envelope and require considerable concentration from its crews", he said.

First sight to concentrate his mind (and everyone else's!) was that of three resident wrecks of a DC-3, a Bulgarian and a Russian An-12, abandoned forlornly beside either end of the runway.

"They were a pointed reminder of what can happen when pilots miscalculate at high altitude airports, caught unawares by the increase of true air speed above indicated air speed", he added.

The whole capability was offered, under the auspices of the United Nations, to the Ethiopian Relief and Rehabilitation Commission which, in spite of the many political reservations, was universally accepted as the most effective famine self-help organisation in the whole of Africa. Gratified that the British Government's gesture had been direct and not through the many relief agencies, with some of whom there had been tension, Commission authorities fell in with a will to provide facilities, sort out day-to-day difficulties and accede to day-to-day requests, sometimes to the extent of quietly standing up to their own Government. Two of these were Col Escheti and Col Tsegaye (later to take over as co-ordinator), both former Ethiopian Air Force Officers who masterminded the link up and pulled it all together, cutting through red tape and bureaucracy and working extremely long hours.

CHAPTER FOUR

Prodding the Dirt

IT was a world away from concrete, navaids and push-button flying, from the luxuries of tower and fire and rescue equipped airfields.

By daybreak on November 5th both Mk 1 aircraft were set to begin a daily routine of three shuttles each. Although grain was building up in the Addis Ababa warehouses, there was a priority to move it from Assab where it was stockpiling in the open. Shipped by relief organisations from twenty-eight countries (the USA, Canada and Europe, in that order, being by far the largest contributors), there it had stuck. Road and rail transport was totally inadequate to convey it to the feeding centres, the people lacking in experience and the country's two poorly equipped harbours at Assab and Massawa unable to cope with the movement of nearly 100,000 tonnes of food needed each month to stave off starvation. They were bursting with undistributed food aid while the monster, drought, threatened to decimate the countryside. Though the Republic of Djibouti had made its port available for un-loading famine supplies, a fifteen mile stretch of road beyond the border on the Addis highway was frequently in rebel hands.

During the first ten days over eighty tonnes were moved from Assab by the two RAF Hercules. It was the start of a daily dawn-to-dusk grind of flying tonnes and tonnes of food to the famine areas, leaving the first-light Garden of Eden beauty of Addis for the moonscape terrain of the hinterland which makes the country such a logistical nightmare.

They found both dirt strips at Makalle and Axum, though not exactly the ideal resting place for a Hercules undercarriage, usable if one ignored boulders the size of footballs. A plea went out for the removal of the rocks and though the locals were slow to start, eventually the rocks were all picked up and taken away. Both strips were over 7,000 feet above sea level, but whereas Makalle had 10,000 feet of once-maintained runway still favourably hard and on a wide plateau, at Axum the 5,200 feet narrow strip was surrounded by high ground, the sugarloaf mountain landmark just a mile from the strip. It was situated on the outskirts of the town, its faded, crumbling gorgeousness once centre of the ancient Axumite kingdon where Christianity was first introduced by the rich and power-

Loading grain on to a RAF Hercules beside the airstrip at Assab. Photo Geoff Whyham RAF

ful Memelik, son of the Queen of Sheba, in the seventh century AD. There was a prevailing southerly crosswind, a bend in the runway, a road at the far end and a resident herd of cows. It was totally unsuitable for maximum all-up weights. There was little space on the primitive off-load pan and extreme caution was needed while taxiing if another aircraft was already on the ground. Because of the proximity of a feeding camp of 10,000 people, strung alongside the runway, folk would pour out towards the landing aircraft and animals were always wandering around. Like a number of Ethiopian airstrips it had a forbidding military area across the runway, opposite the civil side.

Against this, Makalle's grandly named Alula Abanega Airport, although difficult to identify in the dun-coloured scenery, was almost civilised in spite of the downhill gradient of the most frequently used Runway 11 which could strip the tyres unless TAS at that altitude was carefully watched on approach. There was a small ring of refugee tents beside the airfield (later to be disbanded and replaced by a large Italian hospital) and, beyond the town, the two enormous sprawling feeding centres administered by the RRC, the Red Cross and other world relief agencies. It was to become one of the busiest of central Ethiopian airfields with numerous Hercules operators from the West, Soviet freighters and European and American operated twin- and single-engined aircraft either delivering food or loading for onward transportation to remote airstrips.

Asmara, where refugees from the fighting in Eritrea had gathered in large numbers, was the next venue for support flights. Operationally Yohannes IV Airport posed no problems. It has a main asphalt runway of nearly 10,000 feet and a tarmac runway of 6,000 feet, both in reasonable condition. Communications were good and it possessed a workable VOR and DME. But, close to Massawa in rebel-held land, there was no guarantee of safe conduct. However, during early operations, a lot of grain was shifted by the RAF to and from Asmara. Then the Italians, old colonists of the region, based an Italian Air Force detachment at Asmara, and Transamerica, formerly based at Addis Ababa, moved its charter relief base to the north where it was joined by the Belgian and Swedish Air Forces and Air Botswana on the Red Cross and other relief agency shuttles.

Meanwhile, back at Addis Wing Commander Nunn found himself dealing with situations which largely entailed laying a foundation for his successors. Traditionally, an RAF detachment of this size would be led by a Squadron Leader, but because of the delicate political situation it was deemed expedient that an officer of higher rank should be in charge, with a Squadron Leader as deputy.

At first there was unending red tape with stacks of forms and vouchers to fill and be scrutinised, but fortunately the local authorities soon tired of the work involved. Occasionally someone would be pedantic but there were very few times when it was necessary to take a more formal attitude, because of the simple enthusiasm, friendliness and will to pull together of the Ethiopians, from those in authority to local labour. Other international military contingents which, in the course of the next few weeks, arrived in Ethiopia, were all headed by colonels or officers of equivalent rank. The RAF, by far the largest in numbers, must have similar authority should an awkward situation arise.

Barry Nunn's first thoughts on arrival were, of course, the immediate welfare of his detachment, where they would live, eat and sleep, and the establishment of some

sort of headquarters with basic working conditions and hygiene. This was delegated to his deputies and the Medical Officer, Squadron Leader John Merritt. Anxious to expedite immediate air movements, his first task was, with John Morley, to sanction landings on the airstrips.

"It was my final decision where we should go in – or not. Because the need was so great I had to set a series of calculated risk figures, and make sure all those risks were understood", he said.

The RAF's safety record, one of the highest in the world, could not be sacrificed to the heartrending plight of starving people. Bent aeroplanes help no-one. Limits were stretched and wherever it was humanly possible the landings were authorised. The grim tragedy and the need for speedy delivery were uppermost in everyone's minds. Each pilot had to concentrate his mind most meaningfully on getting in safely, fully aware that his masters had no intention of compromising the RAF's record. But there was a tremendous feeling of doing something vital, something terribly important.

Anxious that primitive airstrips serving areas of direct need should be utilised, Colonel Escheti made the RRC's Cessna Centurion available to an international team, including John Morley, to survey strips nearest to some of the largest food distribution centres. Most of these were unlisted and unknown outside the immediate area, with estimates of weight, altitude and temperature all at a critical performance level. Few had been used by relief flights of similar weights and performance. John had the task of not only ascertaining the basic practicality of land-

Beside the airstrip at Axum. People waiting for distribution of food from the airbridge.
Photo by Karel Vervoort, Belgian Air Force

Beyond the airstrip – the 'modern' cathedral built at Axum during this century and a faithful reproduction of the holy edifices which introduced Christianity to Ethiopia in the fourth century.
Photo Ethiopian Airlines

ing on dirt strips that were much shorter and rougher than those normally used by the Hercules, but also of assessing the long-term imponderables. The wave form of uneven runways can set up resonances causing long-term and hidden damage. His detailed survey of each landing strip included prodding the ground with a cone penetrometer to test the solidity of the surface and then assessing the payload-weight that could be safely landed.

The surveys were not always straightforward when every move could be watched with suspicion by bewildered countrymen. One such airstrip was Alamata which served a small garrison town of the same name with large local feeding centres run by the Red Cross, World Vision and various other relief agencies, and was the only strip of any size near Korem. Though both towns had a primitive road system it was more suited to pack animals than to motor transport. At that time the two settlements made up the largest population of distressed people in the

country, and a rapid delivery of food supplies was crucial.

On November 13th John Morley, dumped on his own at Alamata by the Cessna, which promptly disappeared on another errand, found a 3,600 feet usable strip 5,180 feet amsl. Well-meaning locals had in fact extended the strip by 1,800 feet, but he found to his dismay that the extension of the threshold of runway 34 had been made over a dried up water course. Much of the extension was far too soft, pitted and uneven and totally unusable by Hercules. As he prodded the earth and made his deductions he became uncomfortably aware that he was not alone. An Ethiopian, armed with an AK-47, most sinister looking of Russian built hand weapons, was shadowing him. His companion never said a word – just padded after him wherever he went. He said afterwards that he was not quite sure whose side the foreman was on!

It was obvious to him that no large four-engined aircraft had ever landed on the strip's compacted dirt, sand and stony mix – but it would not be the first time that a Hercules had that dubious honour. With his silent follower in tow he poked and paced and prodded. He sketched the rudiments of a landing chart which would become one of every pilot's flight planning documents.

A preliminary sweep of the runway to remove large

stones was required before Hercules operations could begin, and it was clear that surface reliability could change dramatically after heavy rain, especially in its centre. He noticed that the mission light aircraft using the strip landed on runway 34 after flying the circuit, ostensibly to give the people living in a small hamlet at the northern end time to gather up their children and animals. The approach to 34 was fairly straightforward, provided reverse thrust and brakes were effective. Far more complicated was runway 16 with large trees surrounding the village on the approach, some of them thirty feet high and within sixty feet of the threshold. There was also a range of high hills less than two miles north of the strip.

Back in the Centurion (with some relief) he noticed a small green area of land just abeam of what he considered the safe threshold of runway 34. And this small green field, which actually kept its surprisingly refreshing colour, remained the 'threshold marker' for Alamata! He also noticed that the unsafe extended area over the watercourse could be plainly seen to be much darker than the dry dust and stones of the harder area.

So, with short field-landing procedures, a payload about half of that which could be carried into Makalle and a recommendation that landings should be on one side or other of the strip's soft centre, Alamata became one of the most challenging of high-altitude strips for Hercules pilots. And, as with other dusty strips at the height of the drought, they discovered that the very necessary reverse thrust could activate a cloud of dust which would overtake the slowing-down aircraft. Consequently it was imperative to apply reverse thrust immediately on landing and take it off as soon as possible, relying on brakes and the heavy sand itself to bring the aircraft to its taxiing speed.

Ruts at Alamata! One of the most challenging of high altitude dirt strips for Hercules pilots.
Photo author

As the British operation got under way the Russians started flying in to Addis Ababa the first of twelve ageing four-engined An-12 Cubs, pledged to the cause of relief (though equipped with gun turrets!). They set up their line on the pan directly opposite the British detachment, a somewhat sinister presence, operating demurely under the 'Aeroflot' insignia.

Early on November 5th, two days after the British arrival, a West German Luftwaffe contingent of three Transall C-160 military transports of Air Transport Wing LTG.63 staged through Bole for Aba Tenna, the airfield at Dire Dawa, 200 miles east of the capital. During their short stopover in Addis they joined in briefings and their recce pilots were taken on RRC Cessna and Hercules survey flights, as was the Italian Air Attaché, prior to the Italian base at Asmara.

The Germans set up a base at Dire Dawa to operate two of the Transalls on the grain shuttles with a team of fifty strong including four crews (later reduced to three), an operations officer and performance specialist. The third aircraft was held on standby. They were in daily contact with Air Transport Wing headquarters in Munster through the West German Embassy where sanction was given for lifts requested by the RRC and Ethiopian Red Cross.

As the grain started to reach its needy recipients there was soon a shortage of cooking oil. This was speedily remedied with lifts of oil and high protein biscuits (bulkier but not so heavy and more immediately nutritious for the badly malnourished) to Makalle and Alamata. Blankets and tarpaulins, for shelter against the bitter cold upland nights where temperatures could change from 25°C by day to 4°C after dark, were also delivered.

The joint surveys of more airstrips continued. One of the first of these was Gondar about 250 miles northwest of Addis for some much needed early deliveries of food. Flying low level up to Gondar over the breathtakingly beautiful Simian highlands, the Blue Nile falls at Tississat and the sparkling Lake Tana and its many islands with their flocks of coral pink flamingoes, it was difficult to believe that there were problems in this comparative paradise. But famine was creeping up inexorably from the east and the crop of teff, a cornseed millet which was the staple diet, had sprouted in the intermittent rain but remained headless – a tragic negation of hope. It had then been attacked by a plague of 'army worm' caterpillars.

The airfield, which actually boasted an NDB of sorts, was 6,453 feet above sea level with a 4,626 feet usable grass runway approachable only from the south. It was frequently assailed by a cross-or-downwind component and had an extremely hard uneven surface – not exactly the ideal landing place for a large heavily loaded four-engined turbo-prop aeroplane. The first RAF flight into Gondar was only the second heavy multi-engined aircraft to land there, following a L-100-30 Hercules of Trans-america Airlines. An all-up weight restriction of 125,000 pounds had to be imposed, but this did allow for another 10,000 pounds above the restriction at Alamata. All early flights to Gondar carried grain from Addis Ababa.

Two other strips to the west of Gondar and near the Sudanese border were surveyed. These were at Metemma and Humera, both visited intermittently by Ethiopian Airlines DC-3s. The latter was near a poor and remote town of the same name 269 miles from Addis. It was surveyed by a Luftwaffe crew, able to provide a lighter, tighter ship in their twin-engined Transall than a Hercules for a first time landing. Flight Lieutenant Mick Remlinger, one of the British pilots, joined the West Germans for this voyage of discovery.

They found a runway about the same usable length, 3,480 feet, as that at Gondar, on rough black soil full of so many stones that it was suggested that they could be piled up at one end to provide a stopway! Sloping steeply, it had fifteen feet high trees close to the threshold of runway 20, and a tight circuit was necessary to avoid mountains and Sudanese airspace. Mick's cryptic home-made chart warned of 'many shitehawks'. The only suitable parking area was near a collection of tokuls and extremely careful turning was needed to avoid blast damage to the thatched

The RAF Hercules was the first heavy freighter to land at Alamata. This captain landed well to the side of the central ruts. Photo author

roofs. Difficult to find, the crews were recommended to fly up from Addis on the 328 radial and look for a 02/20 dark black strip, making an overhead join as there were no communications. Local people worked hard to clear the stones, lop trees and even remove stumps from the centre of the runway before Hercules operations could be permitted at an all-up 120,000 pounds. After it had been cleared, during those first dry months it was a far more comfortable meeting place of ground and undercarriage than Gondar, where some grief was caused by the rocky surface. When it was discovered that much of the grain delivered to Gondar was shifted to Metemma by mission helicopters, it became the Hercules delivery point for the north-western provinces until its soggy black soil made it unusable in the wet season.

Flying in was one problem, but there was constant fear of landing and finding the aircraft surrounded by rebels. Acutely aware of the situation and still innately suspicious of the West's good intentions, the Ethiopian government decreed that a 'minder' should accompany every flight landing away. In theory this small number of 'security' guards were employees of the RRC. In practice their status was indeterminate. Each arrived carrying a personal firearm ranging from an AK-47 rifle to an out-dated handgun discreetly holstered beneath his anorak and it was generally accepted that they were all henchmen of the Government. Quiet and seemingly inoffensive characters, speaking very little English, when it was explained to them that personal weapons were not permitted in flight on an RAF aircraft they readily released them into the safe custody of the navigator, who returned them to their owners after landing. They soon became accepted, almost as members of the crew, putting in many, many flying hours.

Some airstrips suggested by the RRC were surveyed

and found to be hopelessly unsuitable both in length and substance and surrounding terrain. Their use had to be vetoed. Humera, north of Metemma, recced by John Morley on November 17th, was found to have an ill-defined 3,500 feet runway encroached by vegetation which obscured many of the white stone cairns that delineated its sides, reducing its width in some places to forty-eight feet with a three per cent gradient. Threshold determination was almost impossible because of long grass. Numerous hard obstacles intruded onto so-called 'safety' zones. The only prospect of getting in was on runway 10 with departure on runway 28. To add to the problems were the very close vicinity of the Sudanese border, midday temperatures often over 35°C and much turbulence over the Tekeze river bed. However, John added a note of optimism. A new runway was being built!

The faded, crumbling gorgeousness of Axum and its monolithic remnants of the ancient Axumite kingdom.
Photo Ethiopian Airlines

A world away from the problems of everyday needs – the timeless beauty of King Fasalida's Castle, Gondar. Photo Ethiopian Airlines (bottom)

CHAPTER FIVE

Base Camp at Bole

AIRMEN and soldiers have a unique capacity for turning 'base camp' into a home from home. Prepared to live under canvas, the British detachment set up its tents and field kitchen in a corner of the airfield near the Ethiopian Airlines flying school. However, the RRC, though unprepared for a contingent of this size, found short-term quarters for nearly everyone at the International Livestock Centre for Africa, a research and study centre just twenty minutes car ride from the airport, and the remainder were soon housed in hotels round the city. Space was at a premium at the centre and for some, engineers and RAF police who worked from late afternoon into the night there was at first a 'hot bed' system on a one-up, one-down arrangement. However, the Centre was a pleasant place with a lot to recommend it. The staff catered willingly for such an unexpected influx of boarders and even provided facilities for in-flight catering for thirty-six crew members and mobile airmovers.

"They could not do enough for us. The food was good and safe to eat and there was a swimming pool and tennis court for off-duty guys", Barry Nunn recalled. The field kitchen, tables in the sun which greatly impressed and amused the Ethiopians (there was always the odd butty or cup of coffee for the 'neighbours' when they called by) was used for two months.

The midnight-to-05.00 am curfew, part of everyday life for Addis Ababa residents for the past eleven years, restricted the working day. It meant that local transport drivers working for the detachment could not leave their homes until it was lifted and consequently the first flight of the day could not become airborne until 6.30 to 7.00 am, the second aircraft rolling half an hour later, and both returning, after a long day's ferrying at about 6.30 pm in the evening. At the end of the day engineers and other ground crew toiling to keep a protesting aeroplane airworthy, if they had not finished half an hour before midnight, had to spend the night on the airfield, a chilly and somewhat eerie experience, the curfewed silent hours broken only by the occasional mocking yowl of a hyena, one of a local pack that periodically sneaked down from the hills and across the pan to scavenge among the pickings left on a busy day-time airfield.

The safest and warmest place to doss down for an hour

or two was in the aircraft. However, they were not alone. Three RAF policemen padded the tarmac in their Arctic parkas, keeping guard on the two sleeping Hercules and deserted headquarters, sharing coffee and chat with the local airport security guards who were always keen to practice their English.

Life at 'HQ' in the two tents squeezed alongside the Ethiopian Airlines engineering hangar and another large building in which they were allowed toilet facilities and some storage space, quickly established a routine and took on a business-like atmosphere. In the 'Ops' tent all duties from flight planning to engineering and refuelling schedules were prepared and a telephone was installed. Detachment orders and other useful bits of paper were pinned to boards and flagpoles. Signals home were sent through the British Embassy.

With fairly predictable hot dry weather, the daily flight plans were initiated by the operations officer on the previous afternoon after a visit from Colonel Escheti, communicator of RRC needs and destinations, on occasions a payload Chinese puzzle. These had to be passed by the detachment commander and thrown back to the operations

Main building at Bole Airport, Addis Ababa. In the foreground an Air Botswana L-100-20 is loaded by local workers for a Lutheran World Federation relief centre. Photo Berth Nilsson

officer to sort out payload and fuel quantity, depending on which airstrip was to be used. He then rostered crews in consultation with the captains. His was, in fact, the most demanding of all jobs, arriving at dawn to see off the first flight of the day and leaving long after the last homecoming Hercules had taxied on to the parking area, frequently clocking up a fourteen hour day. Because an all-round knowledge of logistics was demanded, all operations officers were current aircrew from the four Hercules squadrons with two on a one month stint at the same time, on a theoretical day-on, day-off roster – though, like everyone else they frequently gave up the rest day and mucked-in at a moment's notice. They found themselves taking on a mish-mash of tasks neither expected nor experienced within the normal course of duty, from marshalling in a tired Hercules to sorting out some unconventional admin, dealing with a short-notice passenger manifest or calling forward ground transport for people living in various parts of the town.

In the prolonged drought 'getting the weather' was simple, mostly a case of looking across the airfield. One of the historical reasons for drought and desert in many parts of North Africa including Ethiopia is their position on the edges of the Inter-Tropical Convergence Zone, beyond the tropical rainbelts. As the earth tilts bi-annually, first its northern hemisphere and then the south is nearer the sun, evaporating large quantities of moisture from the oceans which falls as rain. Most of Africa gets its rain in one, occasionally two, short wet seasons. Southern Ethiopia can expect a fairly predictable annual pattern. However, Addis Ababa and the north, a land of cool hills and mountains, lie in an obstinate high-pressure zone. The generally static high pressure in northern Ethiopia, while it had the disadvantages of haze, diurnal turbulence and the strong convection currents built up from rapidly heating bare rock and dry soil, minimised time spent on local meteorological facilities, though all relevant documents could be inspected in the tower (some of them quaint copies of CAA pronouncements, printed in Moscow!).

A contract to provide transport was made with the Ethiopian National Tour Operation which provided mini-buses and drivers for the crews and made two cars, both with drivers, available to the detachment commander and his deputy. There was flexible use of all the transport. If the detachment commander's car had a spare seat, it was on offer to anyone who needed it.

The second 'HQ' tent was a welcome haven from working in the burning heat and also from 'Ops' when the afternoon sun came round and turned it into a sweltering hot house. It was also a rest room for the engineers while they waited for homecoming aircraft at the day's end. It housed a fridge, canvas seats and tea-making facilities. Beside it was the water bowser, its contents taken from a nearby tap and daily purified. A field post office was set up with an NCO designated postman, and Ethiopian Airlines were willing carriers.

*   *   *

Western aid from numerous countries, Canada, Belgium, France, Italy, Switzerland, and the United States (to name just a few) was gearing in. Offers of aid had also poured in from Eastern Bloc countries, such as Bulgaria, East Germany, Libya and Poland. The Soviets pledged 300 road vehicles, the twelve transport aircraft and twenty-four helicopters, most of them Mi-8 Hips.

Some movements of the An-12 Cubs seemed to be by night. They were obviously not subject to the curfew! Throughout the year there was a variable line of Cubs, from fourteen down to one or two, just 200 yards across dispersal, brooding on the pan under guard. They came and went on mysterious forays unbeknown to the other airfield occupants.

However, the Russians did move some grain from Assab soon after they arrived, but they were handicapped by their An-12s, not good tactical aircraft, lacking nose

Early days. 'Base camp' takes shape
Photo Stu Bailey

On sentry duties. An RAF policeman and a Bole Airport security guard keep a watchful eye on the parked aircraft. Photo John Upsall RAF

wheel steering and reverse thrust. The maximum load was between eight and twelve tonnes, and their work schedule appeared to be confined to mornings only, with maintenance periods in the afternoon. When they did move grain their turnround was far slower than everyone else's for they refused to allow local labour to help with the loading and unloading, insisting on their own load-masters and movers humping every sack. No-one else was allowed near their aircraft and it could take up to four hours to load a Cub. Perhaps because of their lighter payload, the Soviet aircraft tyres seemed to stand up to the rough runways better than those used by Western operators.

Though they were unpressurised, the An-12s' primary role seemed to be more in troop movement and the con-troversial resettlement programme. There were many stories about the Soviets flying more troops than wheat. Naturally reticent, their crews and personnel were always accompanied by a 'commissar'. Few spoke English and there was at first little communication between them and other people on the airfield. This complicated flying in

the vicinity of the airfield, and British pilots quickly came to the conclusion that there was little listening out in the Cubs. They just seemed to bumble around the sky incom-municado, as and when they felt like it, with buzzard mentality, expecting everyone else to get out of their way.

In Bole tower procedures were further complicated by the presence of a Soviet supervisor whenever the Russians were flying, who tended to over-rule the air traffic controllers. The RAF were in the habit of obtaining VFR clearance into the control zone ten miles out on the DME limit, and using it to expedite landing, a procedure which suited the tower. However, the Cub crews were obliged to fly a full procedural IFR approach, calling 'short finals' at fifteen miles out! Paul Spears had an early experience when the runway was suddenly changed but a Cub was ordered by the supervisor to continue its approach on the former runway, despite the fact that Paul's Hercules was cleared for departure in the opposite direction. He beat-the-hell out of it with a rapid short field take-off and an uneasy feeling that it was safer in the air! No wonder the Cubs were prone to go off the end of the runway!

Air movements at Bole were soon to become chaotic. Not only were relief flights coming in daily but also large airliners from many African nations were flying in packed

Operations officer Flt Lt Hugh Smart, in normal life a 30 Squadron navigator, processes signals in the 'Ops' tent. Photo author

Soviet An-12 Cubs brood in the sunshine under guard at Bole Airport. Between the two aircraft the Soviet 'HQ' can just be seen.
Photo Geoff Whyham RAF

with leaders and officials for the Organisation of African Unity conference, an event of great prestige and importance to the Ethiopian Government, to be held in Addis Ababa. There were some veiled suggestions as to the departure of the British detachment, now down in numbers to seventy after the return home of the small Army set-up team, to Assab or Djibouti. But they held their own – with the backing of the relief authorities. However about a third, most of them airmovers, were turfed out of their comfortable quarters in the International Livestock Centre. They set up a short-term small tented village on the first tee of the golf course within the Embassy compound which was situated in one of the most pleasant areas of the city not too far from the airport. The enclave soon became known as 'Tent City Muppetsville' – and the 'Muppet Flight' even got a mention in *The Times*!

Of far more concern was the noticeable panic among air traffic controllers, more accustomed to the national airline's modest international schedule, a somewhat erratic internal DC-3 network and an Aeroflot service. There was no ground control and they considered themselves stretched if more than two aircraft arrived at the same time. Now controllers of the basic Addis Approach 119.7 and Tower 118.1 frequencies were having to cope not only with the daily increasing relief flights coming

Taking on the precious Avtur. Refuelling at Addis Ababa while the aircraft is loaded for an air land flight. Photo John Upsall RAF

in from all over the world, using them as en route frequencies within 100 miles radius, but with all their important visitors as well. Third World and East Bloc notables tended to believe that they had a right to monopolise radio control for personal messages, as a spokesman for the President of Iraq demonstrated, taking ten minutes to deliver a message over the Tower frequency to Colonel Mengistu, repeating every sentence twice. There was a brief silence from Ethiopian controllers at the end of the harangue until one, not to be outdone, said: "The word you pronounced 'seizing' should be 'seasoning'." The World Vision Twin Otter pilot trying to transmit his outbound call was rendered speechless with hilarity.

Movements at the airport, within the space of two or three weeks, became twenty to thirty times the norm. Before 'perestroika', it was an extraordinary and totally new situation for Western military operators, finding themselves working beside Marxist Leninist air forces and airlines. Though most used English as the universal aviation language, there were those who, through principles or cussedness, did not. For everyone else RT degenerated into basic flight reporting as a self-preservation system.

In overcrowded airspace lacking full reporting facilities there were one or two disturbing air-misses and other incidents. But, to the credit of the civil aviation authorities, they went into action very quickly with an extension of a full three-way monitoring service to detachment headquarters of 'Holloway Radio', a five-megahertz HF radio system, ideal for the ranges involved, on frequency 5536. It enabled the RAF operations officer on duty to keep in touch with the captains of the aircraft and re-authorise them verbally if necessary, wherever they happened to be. Problems could be reported and advice transmitted on this two-way communications system, and with increasing relief flights from world-wide agencies on the famine airbridge, more control was vital. There was a vastly improved separation of aircraft. It made all the difference to peace of mind at detachment HQ, becoming the backbone of communications for the passing on of standard messages between all the relief charters. At Axum and on the strips it was used as a local frequency. Everyone knew each other's estimates and intentions. Another great advantage with the HF radio was that everyone, civilian or military, could be allotted a flight

At Axum the HF 'Holloway Radio' was used by all the western operators as a local frequency. Here a Belgian Air Force Hercules lands on the rocky strip. Photo Karel Vervoort, Belgian Air Force

Home from Home. British Military Detachment headquarters at Bole Airport, Addis Ababa. The LXX Squadron crew, back at base after a day's work, are captain Flt Lt Bob Illet, navigator Sqn Ldr Bob Cumming, flight engineer Sgt Dave Mort, and co-pilot Flt Lt Keith Graham. Photo author

slot with times of departure, ETAs at destinations and return flights – and it began to work well. When there were necessary diversions these could be reported and times revised.

Fuel at Addis Ababa was also at a premium, limiting early RAF flights to three lifts a day. The important conference visitors had priority. However, supplies improved at Assab where it became the custom for the international airbridge carriers to take on fuel while loading. Most of it lacked the sophisticated additives normally used by Western operators which made for easy starting and clean running.

Much of the hoo-haa died down when the OAU conference ended and the dignitaries and their aircraft departed. Even the Russians settled down with most of their flights between Makalle and Assab or other airfields away from famine relief activities. They had a disparate job.

"Everyone did different things at different times", said Barry Nunn who, during his six weeks sojourn as detachment commander, was largely responsible for co-ordinating the flying programme between military and civilian organisations, which was to be followed during the whole operation. Conscious of the taxing demands on both air and ground crews, he devised a flexible and staggered system so that there was an overlap of replacements. Everyone could learn from the experiences of the people they were destined to replace and take over with some knowledge of the conditions and task in hand.

ROYAL AIR FO

ዕርዳታ ማንንዣ
MERCY FLIGHT

CHAPTER SIX

The Muppet Flight

THE British Military Detachment not only donated aircraft and airmanship. They gave invaluable transport logistics, a perfected science of humping weight and bulk from A to B – an area in which the Ethiopians were helplessly, hopelessly inadequate. The RAF brought their own ground support, fork-lifts, flatbeds, condecs and other cargo equipment. Most essentially, they contributed the skills and expertise of their airmovers, many of them veterans of previous disaster relief missions and emergencies, with years of experience of loading and unloading supplies in remote areas such as the Falklands or for flood relief in Pakistan. Other sections, small support units and suppliers, each contributed with one or two men, including the Joint Air Transport Establishment (JATE) from Brize Norton which specialised in logistics.

Most of the RAF airmovers who went to Ethiopia were members of the United Kingdom Mobile Air Movements Squadron (UKMAMS), plus a few from the various static movements sections in the RAF. Formed in 1958 as four MAMS teams, they proved so useful and popular that the eventual fourteen-plus contingency teams found themselves world-wide. There is no doubt that those off-base years of trials and tactical experience helped save many lives in Ethiopia, for these airmen had been involved in every RAF rescue operation since their formation.

Muppets and all! Happy band of airmovers, engineers, suppliers and RAF police on the Hercules roof at Addis Ababa.
Photo Geoff Whyham RAF

The first team included eighteen airmovers and two MAMS flying officers, Colin Waitt and Steve Heaton. Once set up, there was a regular turn-round of about six people who stayed one month. Dubbed the 'Muppet Flight' after its tented exodus to the British Embassy compound, it was subsequently accommodated in downtown hotels, thus solving the bed shortage in the International Livestock Centre.

The cargo was loaded and unloaded and packed into lorries for the short journey from the airstrip to the feeding centres by local labourers. They were supervised by the airmovers, who collated, netted and lashed down the load. They in turn were answerable to the air loadmaster who checked the trim, the weight and balance and position in the hold and maximum permitted weight for the destination airstrip. Payload weights had to be estimated give or take a pound or two. Grain sacks, and not only those filled by local labour, could vary in weight from 100-110 pounds, consequently the payload was an informed guess, within the limits.

In theory manual labour means that air-time is not high. In practice it was very different. Tempting though it might have been to take a purely supervisory role, without exception the airmovers chipped in and lent a hand, their rugged cotton DPMs (disruptive patterned material) mingling with the diverse clothing of the porters on a continuous human conveyor-belt of sacks. Many willing British backs humped food and vital necessities from truck or flatbed or Herky hold in the breathless air of the mountain strips or sweaty heat of Assab. Captains, crew, and even RAF police could be found 'down the back'. However, pilots were quietly dissuaded from the humping operations, on the obvious grounds that a wrecked back could mean one pilot short.

No-one could fail to be impressed with the local porters, the zeal and speed at which they worked and the weights they lifted and carried on their backs and heads. They thought nothing of bearing three or four sacks of grain at a time and under the burden there seemed to be nothing of them but a pair of spindly, malnourished legs staggering along as if by momentum. Even the matchstick children would hump single sacks near twice their own weight, their frail appearance belying their strength. The British airmovers were big, strong and healthy and experienced humpers. But they readily admitted that they were no match for the skinny porters as they staggered along under three or four sacks. There were many friendly weight-lifting contests.

At Assab, from where so much grain was delivered to the hungry by Hercules, local labour became very adept, with the two large truck loads that would fill the hold ready and waiting for the regular arrival flights throughout the day. Sometimes the grain was milled and ready for the cooking pot, and the Hercules cargo bay took on the look of a dusty white mill. Occasionally a sack would burst in the hot dry hold. Loadmaster, engineer and airmovers, stripped to shorts and vests, resembled jolly millers. One crew decided to add a little tone to the proceedings by playing pop music over the public address system. The ice was broken, for the Ethiopians have a hereditary love of rhythmic dancing and they soon contributed their own swaying, foot stamping routine as they passed the heavy, floury sacks from one to another to a monotonous but not untuneful chant sounding like "ub dig baw", which translated, they assured the crew, to "work hard, work hard".

In a moment of spontaneous zeal Master Airloadmaster Bob Jones joined in with his own ritual chant of "Liverpool – Liverpool". The delighted porters added it to their repertoire whenever they saw him (and were soon taught some unprintable variations!). It became noticeable that on occasions when there was no singing and dancing the job seemed to take much longer.

"We were really impressed by the way the Ethiopians helped themselves, loading and unloading quickly and smoothly. At Assab thirty local labourers could unload

Wg Cdr Derek Kingsman, the second British Military Detachment commander at Addis Ababa, discusses the day's schedule with engineering officer, Flt Lt Phil Brown. Photo John Upsall RAF

an aircraft in thirty minutes. A load of sixty pound bales of blankets was shifted in a few minutes", said Bob.

In fact, turnrounds became very brisk. Unloading time at Makalle – wheels down to wheels up – was achieved in twenty minutes. At the height of rescue operations Bole Airport staff were stretched to the limit and RAF air-movers found themselves automatically volunteering themselves and their equipment to unload large air freighters which were arriving daily with enormous cargoes of blankets, trucks, medical equipment and specialised food.

"There was a time when they seemed to be not only loading and unloading ours, but all the other aircraft as well", Barry Nunn recalled.

These ranged from a British Airways TriStar (three flights in an aircraft sold to the RAF and rehired were donated free by the airline to fly direct to Addis with thirty tonnes of medical supplies, blankets, tents and high pro-tein biscuits), two Anglo Cargo 707s from Gatwick, one of them chartered by the *Brighton Evening Argus* full of donated blankets from readers, and two HeavyLift Cargo Airlines freighters, a Belfast and a Guppy, chartered by the American relief agency World Vision and the German Red Cross (one flight bringing in urgently needed Land Rovers). Other 707s from Stansted were chartered by the overseas Development Administration, Save the Children,

and the *Daily Mirror*, its readers donating enough money for supplies to fill two aircraft. Another of the 707s was loaded at Birmingham Airport with food and medical supplies by members of the Aston Villa football team.

Far from being a willy-nilly goodwill operation, much of the European airlift in 707s and DC-8s was master-minded by Relief Transport Services, a non-profit-making organisation based in Amsterdam and Gatwick which drew on international cargo charter airlines where already there was vast experience of delivering supplies to Africa. DC-8s, DC-10s, C-160s from the European air forces and Hercules of Transamerica Airlines and the Belgian Air Force (which was in process of setting up a detachment of two aircraft at Addis alongside the British, to airlift grain for the International Committee of the Red Cross) were also handled by RAF movers. But others, notably from Eastern Bloc countries, were particular about who saw inside their aircraft and laboriously un-loaded their own, with a resultant loss of 'productivity'.

Relief grain began to stockpile in the Addis Ababa warehouses, brought to the capital on the tortuous and obsolete railway from Djibouti, and some, a very limited

Jolly millers. RAF airmovers and crew assist local labourers loading milled flour at Assab.
Photo author

Supplier Sgt Martin McWilliam tallies the spares at 'HQ', Addis Ababa. Photo Geoff Whyham RAF

Ethiopian Government's wariness of Western military involvement meant that the earlier crews were unable to visit the huge refugee camps and feeding stations. Somewhere, out there, were vast numbers waiting desperately to be fed – and all that the servicemen could do was toil, fly, load and unload, conscious of the major tragedy and urgency of what they were doing, but still remote from living contact. Few had failed to see the heartrending scenes of famine stricken families on television, and as they flew north of the city, the arid land of ochre dust below them.

Addis Ababa ('New Flower') is a capital city of two worlds – on the one hand a bankrupt shanty town of unkerbed, potholed roads haunted by homeless beggars, the bulk of its population living in shacks or, if they were a little more fortunate, in the crumbling remains of cool old stucco buildings reminiscent of its ancient and colourful history – on the other a place of pleasant opulence, aping the West it so professed to despise with bright multi-storey hotels and luxurious homes in cool, eucalyptus shaded areas where the rich and powerful lived. British airmen could not fail to see the contrast and incongruity, not least the enormous hoardings in an African city which had shaken off the fetters of a white world but which portrayed as its heroes the pallid faces of Lenin, Marx and Engels alongside the handsome dark face of its own leader, Colonel Mengistu Haile Mariam.

There was a spontaneous appreciation of what was being done by the RAF and invitations flowed which, because of long hours and gruelling days, could be accepted only in moderation. Later, as restrictions were relaxed in a settled routine there was much more fraternisation and freedom and time to visit the upcountry towns and centres and learn at first hand the magical, physical qualities of Ethiopia and its terrible and inherent problems. What the early crews did see were the skinny arms and legs of airstrip and airport workers and their children, picking up the few grains spilt in the hold and round the loading point as the aircraft were emptied, stuffing handfuls into their pockets or pieces of cloth, just for themselves, as if it was gold dust. But it was at the smaller airstrips, such as Axum, that starvation was evident, with the ragged, undernourished people pouring onto the runway from the adjoining camp, their frail arms outstretched in pathetic supplication.

Bob Jones was the first member of the detachment

amount, by road from Assab. It was conveyed in trucks to an assembly point on the airfield near detachment headquarters. This enabled the first RAF Hercules flight of the day, having been loaded overnight, to go direct to Makalle, increasing the daily flights, with three shuttles from Assab, to four. For the airmovers, back at Addis after a long day's flying, there was a cargo of grain to be loaded in preparation for an early take-off the next morning. The days seemed to get longer, at the end of them two very tired Alberts and a lot of very tired men. But no-one even thought of having a grumble.

Just after completion of the first two weeks operation the detachment heard that everyone in the camps round the feeding centres near Axum and Makalle had been fed that day. It was a poignant reminder of why they were there and what was being achieved.

*   *   *

At first it seemed as if the detachment was shielded from the reality of it all. The delicate diplomatic climate and the

Crew members with polybags of clothing and sweets donated by their families to the villagers of Alamata while a cargo of blankets for the feeding camp are offloaded beside the strip.
Photo Geoff Whyham RAF

actually to leave the air-strip and get into one of the feeding centres at Makalle. While the crew was unloading a batch of vehicles destined to shuttle food from the airfield to the centre, one truck developed mechanical trouble. Bob persuaded it to start and his offer to accompany the driver to its destination was gratefully accepted. He bumped along rough tracks through the baked streets of Makalle, the desert capital of Tigre, full of its own harsh 'Arabian Nights' romance with its two ancient Moorish castles and medieval Christian churches, hewn into the rocks. The throngs of people, though obviously very poor, went about their daily toil with resilience and patient resourcefulness. He passed caravans of graceful Arabian camels and gentle asses, loaded with primitive local wares and the main 'cash crop' of the area, rock salt brought west from the Dankali plain and still bartered as currency – and Ethiopian troops, many of them teenagers, camped on the roadside as he approached the settlement. Here it was difficult to believe that the inhabitants were one and the same people.

Not so very long before, they were independently scratching a living in their isolated semi-desert villages and farms. Now, he saw the stark sprawling vastness of the deprivation and appalling physical misery of a once proud people reduced by starvation and disease at just one of the refugee centres. The tents and shelters seemed to extend as far as eye could see. It was a world where a few grains of corn could mean the difference between a life and a death, where water was for rendering that corn into something edible, and not for the washing of sores or skins or clothing. There was that smell of fetid unwashedness and dirt and flies which scavenged on sickness, of hundreds of people, most of them children and the elderly, collapsing and dying every day. There were the bodies distorted by hunger and sad eyes in dark faces that followed him around with silent pleading. His Hercules, when he returned to it, was like a haven in a saner, kinder world. Visibly shaken, he felt that he would be forever marked by that confrontation. There was a strong feeling among members of the detachment, upset by his story of what he had seen, that individually much more could be done. The result was a chain reaction of good-will stretching from Ethiopia's stricken heartland to the towns and villages of the green heart of England.

By November 23rd, just over three weeks after the start of the airlift, the first aircrews began to return home to

Lyneham, to be followed by a gradual replacement of air-movers and ground crew. They had lifted a total of 1,350 tonnes of food and in an average week's flying had set up a weekly schedule of about seventy lifts, moving one million pounds of grain and supplies.

From No. 1 Group headquarters at RAF Upavon Wing Commander Derek Kingsman, who had been acting as 'contact man' between the MoD and the field, joined Barry Nunn on December 5th before replacing him as detachment commander later in the month. He had initiated much of the early preparations and supply for the airlift and it had been originally anticipated that between them they would oversee the completion of a three months operation. He was to stay two and a half months before being replaced. One of his first tasks was to escort Armed Forces Minister John Stanley and a party from the MoD to Assab and Makalle. They were taken to the seaport to watch relief supplies being unloaded at the docks and were also able to tour the settlements at Makalle. They were heartened to see the hordes of families being fed with cooked and wholesome grain delivered by the mercy flights, and the well-behaved little children, clutching their feeding bowls, looking bright eyed and chirpy.

"It made us feel we were accomplishing something", said Derek.

But a visit to some of the clinics told a different story, where health officials and relief missions were struggling to save the lives of later arrivals who had not had the benefits of a few short weeks feeding. For many of them it was just a more comfortable place to die.

"I will never forget it", Derek Kingsman recalled. "There was so much suffering and so little complaint. I have known many African people but the patience and dignity and grace of the Ethiopians will remain with me always. As time went on I think we all felt the same."

John Stanley's report back to Westminster, that not only was the detachment achieving results but that there was still much to be done, swayed the Government's decision to continue for at least another two months. The replacement crews continued the airlift over the Christmas period, seventy men away from their homes and families and carrying on with no let up, quietly conscious that this might just be what the true message of Christmas was all about. But it says much for the civilian population that, at the end of the day, not a single member of the detachment went without Christmas dinner, sitting down with a British Embassy family or as guest of an expatriate household, one of many nationalities.

For Bob Jones and his colleagues, plunged into the festive season of overeating, gifts and glitter, it was a homecoming to feverish activity. They spread the word throughout the length and breadth of the RAF and the Wiltshire towns and villages. A 'Support our Hercules' Ethiopian Famine Relief Appeal was launched by Squadron Leader Ken Bull in conjunction with Save the Children to raise £25,000 for an irrigation scheme to provide fresh water for Bulbulo, a village of 128 families in Wollo province 150 miles north of Addis Ababa, with a pumping system from Lake Haik to seventy acres of farmland. It was capable of expansion by sinking a well at a later date to supplement the water supply, and appealed to the fund raisers because of its long-term benefit. A 40,000 ticket raffle was organised by Flight Lieutenant Roger Davies for a Metro City car supplied at a discount by a Lyneham garage, and over £4,000 was raised by the sale of prints of a sketch of XV187 by Chief Technician John Norris. Publicity of this in *Flight International* ensured a countrywide response.

Post Office Famine in Africa Appeal first-day covers were flown to Ethiopia in a resupply Hercules and carried on an airland flight by a 24 Squadron crew, stamped with the squadron crest and signed by the captain, Squadron

Flt Sgt Roger Clements of 47 Squadron doles out RAF families' gifts to villagers at Alamata.
Photo Geoff Whyham RAF

Leader Angus Morris, Wing Commander Kingsman and Lyneham's station commander, attracting a 'special issue' price.

These efforts were followed throughout the year with a hectic round of fund-raising by members of the various sections and supported by local radio, newspapers and businesses. Over 100 slide shows were presented by Bob Jones to local community groups, and 12,063 pounds of sweets were sent to Ethiopian orphanages. The boiled sweets, the only kind suitable for the climate, were given the thumbs up by medical advisers as a minor calorific addition to the diet and a small treat to brighten the children's lives.

Air Commodore Bill Croydon who, from the MoD, had set the wings of Operation Bushel in motion, was waylaid by his local vicar with a request to fly out some blankets. Expecting to find a bundle in someone's garage he was

An Ethiopian mother and children waiting to be fed at Makalle feeding centre.
Photo Geoff Whyham RAF

confronted by enough blankets to fill eight pantechnicons, the result of an announcement at Sunday service. Though some had to go by sea, needless to say many of those blankets went by Hercules and were soon comforting the backs of deprived Ethiopians against the cold desert nights.

Despite the long hours the detachment found time to adopt two orphanages, the Mother Theresa Clinic in the city and the Debre Segeir Orphanage and Refugee Centre twenty-five miles north of Addis Ababa. They provided 350 metres of two-inch pvc water piping to link the orphanage with its only well and in the city early donations paid for the purchase of two cows, enabling all the children to have a daily ration of milk by Christmas. Birr, the Ethiopian currency, was subject to strict controls and the export of cash prohibited. So a 'penny box' was shoved under the noses of all outgoing personnel to donate their last spare birr to the orphanage as they departed.

Aware that the villagers in Alamata were not entitled to relief supplies (by their own efforts they were comparatively well fed), but really had very little for themselves and felt missed out, the crews delivered clothing and sweets, collected by squadron families for them, one of the numerous small acts of kindness to people they met in the course of the day's work, frequently giving away their own rations of food and chocolate. One MO was heard to mutter that 1985 was the year that the West ruined Ethiopia's teeth!

One day, towards the end of the month, a record airlift of 294,000 pounds of foodstuffs was ferried in eight lifts by the two Hercules. It was to remain a twenty-four hour detachment record.

The decision to continue throughout February was taken. What had begun as a three months famine relief mission was to be extended again and again. The Ministry of Defence had wholly funded the first three months ferrying at £1 million a month, during which over ten million pounds of essential supplies had been delivered to the starving, most to Axum and Makalle, and to Alamata for Korem. With the subsequent extension, even now anticipated as broadly open-ended, it was agreed that the costs would be shared equally by the MoD and the Overseas Development Administration.

A lorry full of grain unloaded from the RAF Hercules and ready for the short journey from the airstrip to the feeding centre at Makalle. Photo author

CHAPTER SEVEN

Labours of Hercules

IF ever a shaggy, unsung truck of an aircraft captured popular appeal, then Lockheed's portly turboprop did with its magnificent contribution to famine relief. It was first manufactured in the mid-fifties for a tactical delivery of troops and cargo into outlandish places. The aggravations of short and rocky airstrips, of flying with its rear end open to the elements and pushing out enormous objects were well known and well catered for in every component. Born in an era of large turboprops, it survived the jet age and has one of the largest production runs in aviation history, proving its exceptional and specialised worth. Fire, flood, earthquake, hurricane, war, landing on Arctic icecaps, supporting the space shuttle launch and recovery – wherever there has been action the Herc has been there, the plump and mousey bridesmaid that no-one gave a second look.

But of course the aircraft had long earned respect, affection and perpetual admiration for its achievements from seasoned Herky watchers and those who worked in and with it – for its payload/range capabilities combined with splendid aerodynamic competence and the strength of a carthorse with the agility of a polo pony. It is a complete pilot's aeroplane, its handling qualities a delight.

There is no doubt that the 'labours of Hercules' in Ethiopia made aviation's most significant contribution ever to saving lives. However, although it was an ideal flying machine for the job, it is doubtful that its designers envisaged such constant landing in such hoary conditions – a daily grind of six or seven hostile meetings of wheels and undercarriage with rocks, ruts, gravel and dust. No previous contingency had punished it, challenged it with quite the same virulence, though previous rescue missions had similarities, and it had come through with flying colours. The RAF had been flogging their aircraft around the world since 1968 when they first took delivery of basically the same C-130H version with its tough Allison T56-15 turboprops supplied to the United States Air Force. But it was designated a 'K' version because the installation of British equipment demanded some divergence of standards. Originally the aircraft had been individually allotted to each of six transport squadrons, four of which became the Transport Wing at Lyneham.

Sixteen of RAF Lyneham's thirty Mark Ones performed

their 'twelfth labour', in the Ethiopian highlands. Sent home to be patched up, like crusading cocks in the pit they returned again and again. Of the remainder of the RAF's sixty-two strong fleet, thirty had become Mk 3 'stretched' versions, deemed not suitable for the punishing short-field operations, nor were they equipped for air dropping. The extra length of fifteen feet built into the central fuselage diminished tactical capabilities and brought the tail section nearer the ground. A long and expensive modification to increase strategic usefulness for load-carrying long-range commitments such as that in the southern Atlantic, was nearing completion. A ravished rear end on top of all the other calculated and uncalculated risks would have been too much.

Preparations at RAF Lyneham. Cpl Kev Brown attaches the Mercy Flight sticker to the Hercules.
Photo Geoff Whyham RAF

In Ethiopia the Hercules flew under Military Operating Standards, disregarding civilian Performance A strictures which are followed in normal peacetime flying. The normal maximum operating weight of 155,000 pounds was increased to 175,000 pounds – more than seventy-eight tonnes all up, if conditions allowed. In the high altitude, take-off compared with a three-engined take-off at sea level heights but without the asymmetric displacement, and it flew just within its own envelope at very high zero fuel weight. It rapidly became apparent that two weeks in the field was just about enough for each airframe at any one deployment. Consequently the weekly resupply Hercules, bringing out crew replacements, equipment and relief supplies, was destined to relieve each aircraft in rotation, though this did not necessarily always happen. Sometimes, if the aircraft scheduled to fly home needed a couple of days' work on it with the new, delivered parts, it was expedient to leave it behind. Tired personnel and spent spares returned in the transitting aircraft. Lyneham was not always certain which aeroplane would return. Later, when one of the two duty aircraft was deployed on air-dropping, there was noticeably less stress, and this enabled the aircraft to be alternated if necessary in the field, though the practice was discouraged by Wing Commander Roger Green, officer commanding Lyneham's Operations Wing, who calculated that the ultimate repair bill might not be quite so horrendous if the number of aircraft deployed on landing operations was limited. A fortnight of operating at such altitudes was taxing enough

without the additions of battered and beaten undersides, shredded tyres, dust ingestion and birdstrikes. In the thin air each aircraft's liquid oxygen supply, ample if based near sea level, could burn off in fourteen days.

The C-130 is so low to the ground that it suffers wear and tear from disturbance, created mainly by the nosewheel. Most returned home minus paint and lower radio antennae at the very least. But its very proximity to the ground also made it the best vehicle for the job, in that no lifts were needed.

At Lyneham each allocated aircraft was given a special 'landing strip' preparation with underbelly, taxi lights and aerials masked in blacktape. The brake pipes were sleeved in quarter-inch-thick rubber tubing and undercarriage door leading edges covered in two or three thicknesses of speed tape (a form of adhesive aluminium). The avionic aerials were protected by two-inch rubberised horsehair which in turn was moulded to the aerial before being reinforced by black sticky tape. Aircraft tyres are normally made for smooth runways, and the first batch were destined for immediate shredding. The entire stock of twenty spare wheels were used during the first week's operation, with engineers desperately waiting for the resupply aircraft. The Hercules damaged

Loading spent tyres at Addis Ababa, part of the entire stock of twenty spare wheels which were shredded during the first week's operation.
Photo Geoff Whyham RAF

Engineers adjust tyre pressure for an airstrip landing. Photo John Upsall RAF

at Axum was grounded for several days and then the second aircraft grounded for want of tyres. It was clear that nothing was going to be straightforward! Paul Spears, thrown in for a second 'blooding' in December when he replaced a pilot who had to return home said: "Though we were aware that tyres were taking a beating I don't think that we really understood what damage those rocks would do. We did not have another burst, but tyres were a limiting factor – we were changing at a tremendous rate."

Whenever there was cargo space Ethiopian Airlines packed Hercules tyres into their London flights – free of charge. Some steel corded tyres were ordered from the USA, and there was a cry for help to Dunlop – was there anything, in the short term, that could be done? Very quickly Dunlop came up with a solution – a reinforcement under the tread but protecting the carcase of the tyre. The toughened tyres were in the field within the first four weeks and were completely successful, some even surviving for retread. There were also some experiments with pressure changes and it was found that if tyre pressure was reduced and oleo strut pressure increased the incidence of shredded tyres decreased. But it was never discovered why, with monotonous regularity, the starboard main undercarriage rear tyres always shredded first!

The first aircraft flew out adorned with the Red Cross logo, an internationally recognised symbol of mercy flights. But the RAF were told in no uncertain terms that as they were not carrying Red Cross supplies they were not entitled to the emblem. Barry went into discussion with Colonel Escheti and the result was the distinctive white transfer with black lettering in English and Amharic, designed by Ethiopian Airlines. It was also used by the West German detachment.

When a Hercules limped home to Lyneham, theoretically a fortnight later, its wheels met the smooth, familiar runway with gentle squeals of delight. There was an extended 'rest' in the hangar while every component was sifted with the proverbial tooth comb. A number finished up in Cambridge for extensive repairs. This meant an assignment to Operation Bushel of at least four aircraft in any one week – one in the Lyneham engineering hangar having its hard graft preparation for resupply, two in the field and the fourth again 'in dock' for recuperation. At the height of the crisis when so much equipment was needed and when air-dropping got underway a fifth Hercules or even a VC10 from RAF Brize Norton was scheduled to resupply, packed with spares and stuff urgently needed at base or blankets or medical supplies for onward transportation. No aircraft left the UK without those boxes and packages pushed into every odd corner – care parcels or oranges and apples for an orphanage, small comforts for a clinic or exercise books, pencils and tennis balls for a little school set up by a struggling mission (not forgetting some beer for the troops!). One early piece of cargo was a large earthmoving vehicle, airlifted on to Alamata and other remote strips which, because of the increased activity and pounding from heavy aircraft, were deteriorating badly. The strips were inspected by a recce pilot after every ten landings and cleared by the earthmover and local manual labour. As the strips improved and undercarriage modifications were implemented, the incidence of damage decreased.

The aircraft were pooled between the four remaining Hercules squadrons, a policy since the Transport Wing was formed in 1970 and based at Lyneham. The squadrons, 24, 30, 47 and 70 (the latter traditionally known by the Roman numerals as LXX) all saw the light of day during the First World War. All played their part in Operation Bushel. Each month one of four crews was provided in rotation between 24 and 30 Squadrons. The remaining three crews came from 47 and LXX Squadrons. Initially all four operated on air-landing details, but as soon as air dropping was sanctioned it became the task of the two latter squadrons. This was because of the basic differences in role and training. In recent years the 'route boys' of 24 and 30 Squadron had specialised in long range flying, air-to-air refuelling and the needs of Falkland Islands support with short haul, short strip flying but a small part of their day-to-day operations. However, they more than held their own with the two tactical squadrons where efficient 'gumshield' delivery of the goods on outlandish airstrips were concerned, taking over much of the strip flying when air dropping started.

Historically the two tactical squadrons were no strangers to Africa. They had served in the area since the early 1920s when 47 Squadron policed desert areas for the Sudan Defence Force and, during the Second World War bombed Italian airfields in Eritrea from somewhat obsolete Wellesleys which were based in Asmara. It became the first transport squadron to be equipped with Hastings and fly in coal during the Berlin Airlift to keep the city's mainstream going until the blockade was lifted, one of many rescue missions. LXX Squadron saw intense activity from numerous bases in North Africa and the Middle East during wartime, in the late 1940s and during Suez operations when its Hastings dropped parachute troops on Port Said. Past skills made the squadron experts in a modern role. For during the past decade the air dropping of stores in large weights and quantities had become highly professional and specialised, needing constant rigorous training. Consequently the two tactical squadrons had concentrated on air despatch and their efficiency in these methods of delivery had come to be recognised as the best in the world.

* * *

The success and very low grounding rate of the Hercules under such extreme conditions says much for the devotion of aircraft engineers who kept the turnround going at home, at base and in the field. Before leaving Lyneham they had foreseen just about everything that could go wrong and the spares needed to be either available in Addis Ababa or carried on every sortie. For engineers based at Addis Ababa there were exceptionally long and unsocial hours as the two homing aircraft landed, one after the other in the late afternoon. The hours of waiting in the stuffy shade of headquarters canvas were suddenly transformed into a sweatshop of activity with a cry of "Here's Albert" as the reverse thrust roar of its four

Warrant Officer Paul Foley (a member of the 47 Air Despatch Squadron advance party) chats with Birani, an RRC labour supervisor at Bole Airport, Addis Ababa. Photo by John Upsall RAF

Allison turboprops echoed and surged with a sing-song change of tone while the undercarriage rocked on the switch-backs and varied gradients peculiar to the threshold of Runway 07. Then there was a general exodus onto the pan to marshal in their charges each to its own tight parking area.

In addition to everyday maintenance which had to be carried out before, during and after flight servicing, considerable extra time had to be spent inspecting the tyres, underbelly fuselage, undercarriage doors and lower avionic aerials for stone damage, adding hours to an already lengthy procedure. Stones the size of cricketballs were sometimes removed from the undercarriage after landings at Makalle or Gondar, even though it was protected. All the protective material had to be inspected and repaired on or after closing down checks. It was a perpetual grind of mend and make right. So much grain embedded itself in the hold that there was a standard joke that it would soon have to be mown! After air dropping started it all became a continuous round from mid-morning when the aircraft returned from the first drop of the day and was checked and patched during reloading.

A ground engineer flew into each strip as a member of the crew. Aware that landing speeds at high altitudes could be close to the nosewheel tyre limiting speed of 137 knots, he made an extensive inspection after each strip landing run. Makalle's downhill runway was famous for stripping bits off tyres. A tyre and undercarriage bay check was carried out while the aircraft was being unloaded and it included taxiing forward a foot or so to complete the inspection of whole tyre areas, climbing onto the wheel bays with brakes and chocks on. Incoming engineers were briefed on the procedures for checking the reinforced tyres, and advised not to snag an aircraft for the odd worn tyre edge. It was dubbed the 'Little Rock Brief!'

In the very early days, unsure of operational conditions and to minimise risks of getting stuck away from Addis Ababa, they had loaded and unloaded with engines running. This produced problems of heat, dust and noise and difficulties in communication, and after about three weeks was discontinued. All vents and bleed valves had to be closed for strip take-offs, landings and taxiing to minimise dust ingestion. This could be enormous while reverse thrust was being used, the cloud of sand and soft gravel catching up and enveloping the slowing down aircraft in a dirty 'pea-souper'. Whenever possible, and especially at Assab where the wind was a constant thirty to forty knots, the aircraft was parked into wind with oil

cooling flaps opened and all electrics not needed switched off to avoid overheating. There was always a lot of people milling around and wings and fuselage had to be monitored most carefully.

In addition to damage expected on rough landing strips there were the all-too-frequent birdstrikes, a continuous hazard to both large and small aircraft. There were incidents of a vulture hitting the starboard wing of a Hercules on take-off at Addis and of another vulture finishing up at the co-pilot's feet. Shortly after Ray Bond's multi-confrontation at Rabel a multi-birdstrike was experienced by another pilot, Flight Lieutenant Martin Oxborrow, while landing at Makalle. It caused a four-inch dent in an external fuel tank. A large roll of speed tape and a plentiful supply of filler were standard issue to every mobile engineer, and if holes and dents were minor, they were patched up on the strip. Patching up resolved itself into a team effort with the engineers backed up by the 'loadie' (most of whom had practical engineering experience), airmovers and crew, with willing, if unskilled, local volunteers.

There were the inevitable small dramas. One late afternoon at Assab a starter shearing collapsed – in ideal conditions a repair job of several hours. The team toiled on in the sticky heat as the light began to fail, the grain sitting in the cargo bay. With local talk of fighting in the vicinity, the captain (again the resourceful Flight Lieutenant Spears) knew that it was imperative to get airborne before nightfall. By the time the repair was completed the

Worm's eye view of damaged tyres and undercarriage after a strip landing.
Photo Southern Air Transport

Open door flying in predictable clear blue Ethiopian skies for a RAF Hercules. Photo Jim Gilchrist

desert airfield, unequipped for night movements, was pitch black.

The hero of the hour was indisputably Paul Foley, a warrant officer of 47 Air Despatch Squadron familiar with local conditions. He emptied ten compo-ration tins of their contents and set airfield workers to fill them with sand and rags soaked in aircraft fuel, and also persuaded a couple of drivers to take their trucks to the end of the runway where their flashing headlights would mark the limit. Paul Spears vividly remembers his eerie take-off.

"When we were ready to roll the Ethiopians raced down the runway and lit the cans. But there was a bump in the runway and I couldn't see a thing. Paul was urging me to start rolling for he estimated the flares would burn for only two minutes. So I put on power and suddenly, over the hump, the brilliant flare path became obvious."

As they set course overhead the flares were still burning, a weird, flickering, fading light.

A more serious mechanical problem had to be solved by a second aircraft flying in to the rescue. Between Makalle and Assab one engine produced an oil leak.

Once on the ground the engineer could not find the source and there were fears that a ground crew would have to be flown up from Addis to carry out repairs. However, the other Hercules was diverted in flight to go to its aid and when the engine was topped up with the two aircrafts' spare oil supplies and run on the ground, it was decided that it was airworthy. It arrived back at Addis still on four engines, was rectified and tested, ready for work the next day.

Major birdstrikes usually entailed a major replacement, such as an engine change or a new wing leading edge. The resupply aircraft was always full of bits to fix the aircraft in the field and also the returning aircraft, which was not always in an immediately flyable state. It sometimes had to be patched up first, either for the return flight or to continue airbridge operations – consequently those on the home-going passenger list were never quite sure of take-off day or time. Serious airframe damage resulted in the aircraft being withdrawn from operations and a delay while it was patched up for the long hop to Akrotiri, where engineering facilities were more sophisticated, and then the flight home to Lyneham or Cambridge for an extended lay-off.

In spite of the many vicissitudes, the aircraft remained

comparatively trouble-free. Only three engine changes were necessary during the whole operation and as time was extended a spare engine was positioned at Addis and kept 'next door' in the Ethiopian Airlines hangar, alongside a Transamerica spare engine which had been left behind at Addis when the charter airline moved to Asmara. This had been frequently robbed by the 'Brits' and left with an IOU on its denuded area until the parts were brought out for replacement in the re-supply aircraft.

There was exceptional co-operation from Ethiopian Airlines engineers. They had extensive workshops and were very innovative, much to the detachment's admiration. If they did not have an aircraft spare, they made it. Nothing was too much trouble for their next door visitors and a lot was quietly done, with no haggling and no talk of cost, for much of it went unrecorded. RAF engineers were most impressed with their motivation and efficiency. As one said: "I would fly with them any time." What better accolade from engineers of reputedly the safest transport airline in the world!

As a passenger transport the Hercules has a reputation for being safe, uncomfortable, slow, cold and noisy. A plentiful supply of earplugs is standard loadmaster's equipment. There is little communication among fellow travellers, a very restricted sign language at best. The heating system on some of the aircraft can be erratic – turn it up and the human cargo is panting, turn it down and there is a scramble for woollies. The red canvas bucket seats lining the inner fuselage are marginally better than a hard bench.

But for most members of the detachment, from the chilly clamber on to the aircraft in the early hours of one murky English dawn to when, mission accomplished, their feet found the Lyneham tarmac again, it became a sort of 'semi-residential satellite', a haven far away from home. Seasoned 'Ascot Airline' passengers, they had long developed a low cunning, armed with ear defenders, cushion or sleeping bag, with an eye for a convenient foot-rest cargo ledge at seat level. If the aircraft was packed to its limits, there was very little leg-room. Once airborne, the really blasé veterans rolled up in their sleeping bags along vacant seats or on top of the cargo, whiling the droning hours away in blissful oblivion, or they slung cargo nets as hammocks under the cargo door – by far the best way to travel if one was not actually flying the aircraft! If a vehicle was among the freight, a front or back seat was commandeered by the crafty.

There were other manifestations of the general home-from-home atmosphere, such as damp towels or even rinsed through more intimate apparel drying on the well cladded roof area piping. Sometimes, on a homebound flight with comparatively few returning spares or baggage, there was space to walk around and stretch legs, a luxury indeed. And even the most critical of passengers could not fail to respect the Hercules' winged truck stability as it ploughed through the skies. Understanding aircrew were generous in allowing a few passengers at a time a welcome break on the flight deck.

The sixteen RAF Lyneham Transport Wing C-130s which operated on the Ethiopian airlift were: XV178, XV181, XV182, XV186, XV187, XV191, XV205, XV209, XV215, XV292, XV293, XV295, XV297, XV299 (now a Mk 3 Hercules) XV300, XV306.

Setting course overhead in drifting dust after a successful air drop at Rabel.
Photo John Upsall RAF

CHAPTER EIGHT

'Tesfa'

CONVINCED that air-dropping food was the most effective way of saving people from starvation, especially where there were no landing strips, the RAF left no stone unturned to persuade the Ethiopians of the effectiveness of the heavy free-drop system which had proved so successful in the famous 'Khana Cascade' in Nepal in 1973 and 1980, even though the technique was not normally practised by the RAF. However, the circumstances were similar. Air drops from Hercules had delivered some 2,000 tons of desperately needed grain to starving villages in inaccessible Himalayan foothills in a race against time before the monsoon started. There the crews had packed and loaded in high temperatures and despatched at heights up to 10,000 feet above sea level, completing the mission in one month.

From the earliest days of Operation Bushel, Barry Nunn had consistently stressed the benefits of air-dropping and received an enthusiastic hearing from Colonel Escheti, the RRC's commonsense co-ordinator. But the Ethiopian Government shied away. They were afraid that proper control and distribution of supplies would be impossible – that food would scatter willy nilly and that it would get into anti-government hands, or that there would be punch-ups over it, culminating in the survival of the fittest. Past experience had shown, world-wide, that where air-drops had been made by well-meaning but disorganised agencies and food just dumped with no radio or human control this is what had happened. There were already reports of western aid, given unsupervised by various governments, straying into the hands of rebel troops. They could not believe that any system of control would be successful.

Air Despatchers sorting sacks for rebagging for a test drop at Bole Airport, Addis Ababa.
Photo 47 Air Despatch Squadron

Trial drop at Addis Ababa on grass beside the main runway from XV 215 before the first air-drop at Rabel on January 26 1985.
Photo John Upsall RAF

So far all nations which had contributed aerial assistance had answered a call to carry food quickly and in bulk to assembly and feeding centres, and while the Ethiopian Government were aware that people were deserting their farms and land to come to the centres to be fed, they could not see a viable alternative.

At first there had been a total unpreparedness for the massive inrush of supplies which had come after a decade of relative neglect. Emergency food aid, dumped in the open at docks and airports, had piled up without the lorries, trains and aircraft to get it to the starving. Chartered ships and aircraft were not paid to sit about and air-cargo handling facilities which were often limited at bases and ports, were swamped. Bulk cargo, lying on the quayside or in a corner of some airfield, not only tested security but quickly deteriorated from the attentions of rats and birds. So all assistance from foreign military and civil airlines had concentrated on clearing the ports and delivering it to areas where population and need were greatest. The initial crisis was being solved as far as possible by the daily air-land shuttles, though in fact the camps were serving less than half of the starving population.

But it was becoming clear that a different emergency situation was looming. The long awaited rains, due in May, would cause problems not yet experienced by the relief missions flying large aircraft. The dry and dusty strips would become seas of mud and water, and flying conditions in the highlands, enveloped in low cloud, a vast change from the predictable high pressure weather so far encountered. It was obvious that air-landing operations could be seriously curtailed. In the worst of the famine areas there was no-one on the deserted farms to plant the season's crops or till the land. Instead, they were gathered in immense unhealthy congregations where cholera, TB and measles were rife, entirely dependent on handouts – a no-hope situation without any planning or incentive to help themselves in the longer term.

The reluctance to return was understandable, an apathy caused by malnutrition and memories of sowing seeds and harvesting dust, and lost incentive and independence under forced collectivisation. Four years of drought coupled with Marxist incompetence had reduced crops overall to thirty per cent, killed 500,000 people and caused 500,000 more to trek 300 miles west into Sudan. In the Ethiopian refugee camps the million mark had been passed. The choice had been starvation at home or a desperate, sometimes fatal, journey to a feeding settlement. But more than lives were being destroyed –

the very social and economic fabric of the country, by which Ethiopia lived and fed itself, was disintegrating.

Derek Kingsman took up the cudgels that Barry Nunn had handed on to him. "Until now there had been no urge to go back and work the land. Most were still too weak for a long trek home to empty storehouses and the effort of planting. Their oxen, which normally pulled the plough, had all died in the drought or been eaten. But if food was dropped to them in their villages so that they could be strong enough and ready to make a fresh start before the drought broke – this was a different story."

He added: "It seemed to me that in the rainy season when airstrips and roads were washed out, air-drop could be crucial."

The RRC, as anxious as everyone else to resettle people so that once more they could be self-sufficient (especially in Northern Shewa, within 150 miles of Addis Ababa, where they were less likely to be manipulated by rebel factions), was beginning to have second thoughts. Kurt Jansonn, the UN's Assistant Secretary General finally convinced the Ethiopian Government that air-dropping was not only necessary but that the British and West Germans, who would carry it out, had no political axe to grind and were only there to do a good day's work. Another strong advocate of air-dropping, who had been seconded to the UN team in Ethiopia was Staffan de Mistura, a Food and Agriculture Organisation expert who had been involved in

successful air-dropping in Chad when carried out by the French. He was able to explain the advantages – and agreement was achieved after weeks of political hiccups.

The RAF had already convinced the British Government, which at first had expressed reservations on such an operation. Briefings were given to Timothy Raison, Minister for Overseas Development and Administration and also to officials of Oxfam and Save the Children. An air despatch demonstration was set up by No 1 Group at Upavon for Press and television on Salisbury Plain and a training exercise free-dropping four tonnes of grain donated by Wiltshire farmers (instead of the gravel normally used for training) was held. This was watched by a contingent from the MoD and representatives of companies and firms which had offered equipment. It was an eye-opener to the sceptics.

Wing Commander Brian Nicolle, LXX Squadron's commanding officer recalled: "The trials were held primarily to re-test techniques used in Nepal and the latest container systems. We knew that the lush green Plain in January was very different from the stony, mountainous drop zones. However, we pulled out the old Nepal reports and blew the dust off them, and consulted people who were there".

A Luftwaffe Transall fitted with an automatic despatch system took part in the trials.
Photo Jim Gilchrist

The Mk 1 Hercules was flown by Support Training Squadron Instructors, with a team of four soldiers from 47 Air Despatch Squadron. The unique Army-Air Force partnership between the two tactical flying squadrons and the tiny Army squadron of 120 soldiers had built up a reputation for being the best in the world. Though labour-intensive, they were still the most accurate, beating USAF crews and other international air forces with much more sophisticated automatic systems in general competition. The small section of the Royal Corps of Transport's elite flying soldiers was heir of the Air Despatch Group formed during the Second World War when its major activity had been the delivery of 600,000 tons of stores into Burma in 1944 (three times the tonnage of RAF bombs during the great offensive into Germany!), and of 749 Air Despatch Company which handled much of Britain's involvement in the Berlin Airlift. They had specialised in air-drop and heavy-drop techniques, mostly with the use of parachutes. At their Lyneham headquarters, heavy supplies including vehicles were broken down into manageable lots, packed into suitable containers or onto platforms and despatched in flight to receiving units on the ground. An air despatch crew of four, led by a corporal, was an integral part of the aircraft's crew. In addition some members of the squadron were trained to set up a supply drop zone with markers and radio and to distribute supplies, landing by parachute if necessary.

Proud of his little squadron, its commanding officer, Major Terry Lewis said: "They are accustomed to working all over the world with other services, and are ambassadors for their Corps, the Army and their country. They are tough, intelligent, benevolent and dedicated."

In Ethiopia they were to more than prove his words. The aircraft and the flying skills were already there. On their expertise rested much of the success of the biggest and most consistent air-dropping operation they had ever undertaken.

Meanwhile flyers and despatchers were putting their heads together to reflect on lessons learnt during the Khana Cascade (so named by the Nepalese – 'Khana' means 'food') and how the free-drop system could be utilised in Ethiopia. The 'Khana Cluster', a collection of sacks with an all-up weight range to 2,400 pounds lashed to a pallet with cord and sent down the aircraft cargo bay on a roller conveyor to the edge of the ramp where it was heaved out manually, was used for the demonstration.

The major problem in air-dropping had always been the survival of the dropped item in one piece. The right sort of container, in this case a sack, and packing it correctly, was vital to the operation. The baseboard not only acted as protection and centre of gravity but was also an aerofoil in itself, though it usually broke up on impact. The tough jute UK-made military issue sacks were used in the trials and also some from local sources. It was found that survival improved if the corn was triple bagged, and the bags were half filled to allow for a vacuum, that there was a balance between making the most of each cluster in terms of grain delivered and having the sacks burst at the seams on impact. The right tension in the lashings was also important – too tight or too strong and they would cut into the sacks and fail to allow separation when the sacks hit the ground – too loose or too frail and they could fall apart prior to despatch during handling.

There was a great deal of enthusiasm from members of the public, all eager to help. One man sent in copious diagrams showing his scheme for the operation of giant bouncing footballs full of supplies which would be aimed at and stopped by trees. Another suggested winged packages shaped like sycamore leaves and insulated by silver paper which would flutter to the ground as air was extracted.

*   *   *

Confident that the green light was about to be given for air-dropping Wing Commander Kingsman called forward a team of despatchers, sacks and baseboards to arrive in the resupply aircraft on January 22nd. Such was the enthusiasm that it seemed as if half of 47 AD were on the manifest.

"I was horrified at the numbers, for accommodation was critical. I signalled home that we were there to assist the Ethiopians, not invade them!" he recalled.

The major problem in air-dropping – the survival of the sack in one piece. Photo Jim Gilchrist

He set up an 'international' tent on the airfield, near an assembly point where the grain would be rebagged for air-dropping. Here, the collaborators met. The Luftwaffe were as keen as the RAF to free drop. They had practised it with some success in the Sudan and had their own palletisation equipment. Their seventy-six tons Transalls were fitted with automatic despatch systems whereby the rear half of the load was shunted on to a canvas which released the pallets at a flick of a switch, operated by two loadmasters. It was not as accurate as the manual system and not as easily rectified if things went wrong. It had not originally been designed for free dropping and was suitable for only two drops in any one flight. However, each aircraft could carry seven pallets, each weighing a ton and loaded with forty sacks. With a smaller, lighter aircraft than the Hercules, flying purely by radar altimeter with the engineer calling the height, they were able to drop from fifteen feet above the ground, using ten degrees of flap with gear down. On the second drop they were able to bring the speed back to 120 knots.

The day after the arrival of the British air despatchers (three crews each of four men) and their equipment, some joint demonstrations were held at Bole Airport before RRC officials, relief organisations, the Belgian Air Attaché and the British and West German ambassadors to Ethiopia – to prove to them that air-dropping was feasible. The trials were held over an expanse of grass between the terminal and the runway, opposite the RRC office. A Luftwaffe Transall was flown in from Dire Dawa by Major Volker Heinz specially for the trial. The Hercules, XV191, was captained by Flight Lieutenant Jim Norfolk, an instructor with the Support Training Squadron at Lyneham and a 47 Squadron crew. Each aircraft made four separate passes.

Wing Commander Nicolle, destined to be the next detachment commander and already in Addis Ababa, said:

"Again, it was an experiment with bags. The local sacks were of poor quality and we quickly decided to go to our own resources. We tried different combinations and found that using three sacks – splitting the grain into two small sacks inside one large one – gave us between eighty and ninety per cent success. I felt it should be more but the UN were happy with an eighty per cent success rate."

It became apparent early on that the British method of packing, stacking and despatching was by far the superior system. The locally made jute sacks, used on the first drop by both operators, resulted in much of the grain being spilt as the bags burst on impact. Placed inside the nylon ballistic sacks for the second run in, the results were excellent. About twenty white sacks were dropped from the Hercules, each roughly 110 pounds on eight thick plyboard sheets, two at a time, from about fifty feet above ground, at a groundspeed of 140 knots, very close to the aircraft's true airspeed minimum. They landed very close to the target, one cluster actually demolishing the sheet which marked the spot.

But nothing was to be straightforward. Having got the political will to trial drop, before air-dropping proper could go ahead helicopter support was vital. In that dramatic terrain a very comprehensive survey of each drop zone, selected by the RRC as the area in most need, was imperative. A landing party was necessary for each day's operation to set up the radio and ensure that conditions were suitable and safe for air-dropping.

A meeting was arranged with the Soviet military authorities. This took place in the terminal building – their delegation headed by a general.

"We made a deal", Derek Kingsman said. "They would provide helicopter support with a Mi-8 Hip. The meeting was held at 11.00 am with apparent agreement, hearty handshakes and smiles all round but by five o'clock the same afternoon the offer was withdrawn."

A second meeting with the Russians had the same result, their excuse being that they had had two recent accidents, the aircraft were unserviceable and they declined to take passengers. There was a strong impression that individually the Russian crews wanted to help but that Big Brother said 'No'. However, temporarily, the problem was resolved. Anxious that the project should not fail, the Ethiopian Air Force, which had only two helicopters of the same type based at Addis, made a trial offer of support.

The area chosen by the RRC for the first air-drop was near Rabel in northern Shewa, 100 miles northeast of Addis Ababa, on a plateau over 9,000 feet above sea level surrounded by deep ravines and gorges where 175,000 hungry mountain dwellers lived. On January 26th a 47 Squadron crew comprising pilots Flight Lieutenant Jim Norfolk and Flight Lieutenant Graham Watson, navigator Flight Lieutenant Martin Stringer, Engineer Sergeant Ian Parker and Master Airloadmaster Eric Brakes, with two air despatch crews, made the first heavy free-drop in the whole relief operation, from Hercules XV215.

It was the start of the biggest air-drop operation ever performed by the RAF and the Luftwaffe. The UN dubbed it "Operation St Bernard", but the Ethiopians named it "Tesfa". It was their word for "hope".

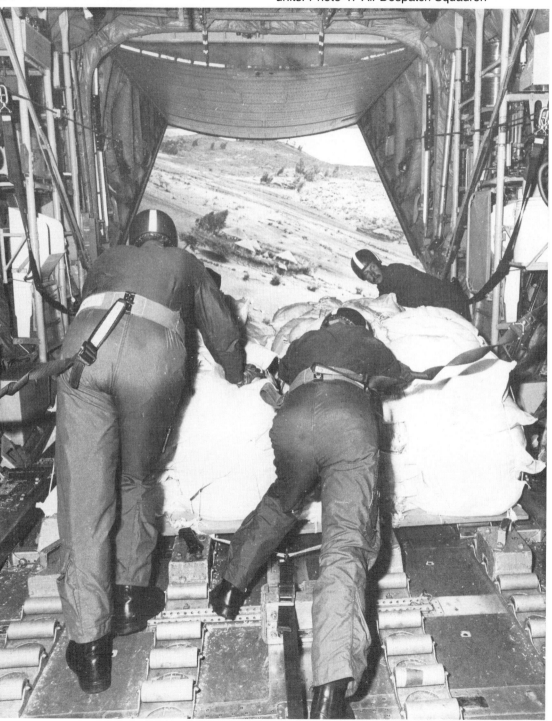

'Clear live drop'. The start at Rabel of the biggest air-drop operation ever undertaken by the British military partnership of RAF and Air Despatch units. Photo 47 Air Despatch Squadron

A no-hope situation. Starving people at the World Vision relief camp at Alamata. Photo MAF

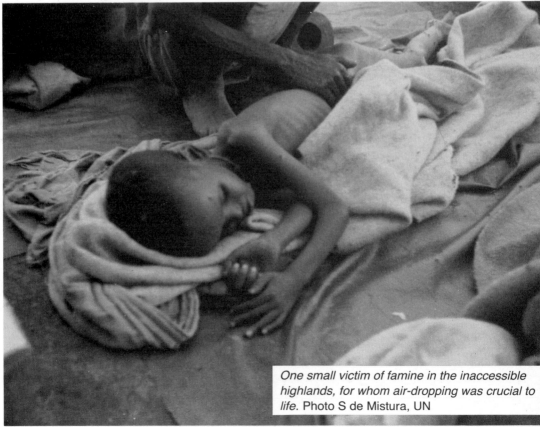

One small victim of famine in the inaccessible highlands, for whom air-dropping was crucial to life. Photo S de Mistura, UN

Tips from an air-drop veteran. Flt Lt Jim Norfolk (left) hands over to a successor, Flt Lt Chris Dark, from 47 Squadron. Photo John Upsall RAF

CHAPTER NINE

Clear Live Drop

NO other drop-zone could have tested the crew to their limits and proved their expertise to a waiting world as did Rabel. Near the Wollo borders, it was wild, beautiful and, at low level, quite hair-raising. Situated in the shadow of a ridge, the approach had to be flown in a curve, levelling the wings only just before reaching the release marker. The drop zone was tiny, a power-off run-in on 240° magnetic over the small plateau which had a fairly steep downhill incline ending in a sheer drop, and then a turn right onto 274° immediately after dropping in order to avoid a hill, the banking starboard wing tip just a few feet from the ground.

The DZ had in fact been looked at by a Hercules crew earlier in the month, with a recommendation that the run-in should be in the opposite direction because the approach looked less complicated. But this was vetoed by Brian Nicolle who considered the steep uphill gradient and high ridge beyond it too dangerous. His point was soon proved when one of his captains, Ray Bond, suffered a multiple birdstrike and lost an engine over Rabel.

The day before the drop, despatchers and air crew had flown with Colonel Escheti to the DZ in one of the Ethiopian Air Force helicopters for a survey and to chart the zone. On the day of the drop the helicopter preceded the two fixed wing aircraft with an air despatch landing party who set up the radio and markers. The local officials had already been warned to keep the area free of their own people but, needless to say, there was much curiosity and folk from the small town about ten miles away, swollen by hungry nomads, perched in many hundreds on the rocky outcrop.

The first drop was made from the RAF Hercules and the second from a Luftwaffe Transall. Both demonstrated a satisfactory and efficient way of delivering food to remote areas. There was an eighty per cent success rate with the British sacks. On the second run-in, because of midday turbulence, both aircraft were forced to drop from a greater height with marginally less success, especially the Germans, whose sacks were less durable. One of their loaded pallets was lost when it fell in a gorge.

As the second aircraft banked and turned for base the swarms of people descended on the DZ to hump the precious grain to the distribution centre in the town.

It had been planned that a large international Press and television coverage would record the event, but with space in the helicopter limited they set off by road and, as was half expected, the 'road show' did not arrive until three hours too late. An American NBC crew managed to get themselves smuggled aboard the Hercules and obtain an early scoop.

Anxious that all sides of the political curtain should see the results, Staffan de Mistura persuaded the Ethiopians and the RAF to take up the Press party the next day when the Hercules crew put on a repeat performance (the Germans declined, feeling that they had not quite got their act together regarding sacks and packing). A successful Hercules air drop was seen on the world's television screens.

As Jim Norfolk commented: "It was an unusual exercise and we were rather busy. But in the back they seemed to be thoroughly enjoying themselves."

But expectations were shortlived. Regrettably the Ethiopians withdrew helicopter support. One of the two Hips based in Addis was the Ethiopian Army Commander-in-Chief's personal transport – and there was still government concern about control of supplies. The RRC officials then said they would prefer to have small packets of food dropped over various areas each day.

"I had to convince them that maximum advantage could only be had if one zone was filled with one month's supply from continuous sorties", said Brian Nicolle. "As a zone became familiar, our crews got their 'eye' in and dropped more accurately – and I could afford only one DZ party."

Frequent meetings to try to resolve the impasse were held between detachment commanders, Colonel Escheti and representatives of the RRC, the UN, and the Luftwaffe. There were veiled threats that valuable resources were being wasted and that if things did not get going soon air despatchers and their equipment would be sent home. More pressure was brought to bear by the UN and also by a number of ambassadors, including the Polish Ambassador Andrej Konopacki. He was asked by the Ethiopian government to provide help.

Like a breath of fresh air, the small Polish relief helicopter squadron breezed in. It was the missing piece of jigsaw, setting up camp under canvas at Lidetta with three Mi-8 Hip helicopters, already painted white with the red cross and red circle of mercy for the start of a ferry of

Map of the drop zone at Rabel – drawn by the crew on a survey helicopter flight the day preceding the drop.

RABEL DZ	10°31'N 39°34'E
ALT 9020' AMSL	ADDIS 025°M /100nmk
RUN IN 250°M	RH cct Escape 275°M

DEACON TANGO 246·7

N

HIGH GND

S nm

ROUGH GRND

DOWN SLOPE

TRENCHES

50ˣ 200ˣ ⊗

250°M

VERY SMALL DZ 250ˣ LONG 200ˣ WIDE

HIGH GRND WITH TUKULS

health workers and small clinics to remote areas. The squadron of twenty-two air crew and engineers was commanded by Colonel Kazimierz Pogorzelski. At Lidetta they shared the military airfield with a number of East Bloc visitors, few of whom were on relief work.

A Polish flight engineer cleaning filters after landing at a dusty DZ. Photo author

POLISH RELIEF
HELICOPTER SQUADRON in ETHIOPI

The Polish crews were unfailingly efficient, hard working and cheerful, ready at first light to transport the air-despatch landing parties to whichever drop zone was allocated, searching it out, sometimes taking over some of the landing party duties or supplying the radio, flare gun or markers. They flew by the seat of their pants, mountain hopping 'as if on a tightrope' between ridges, as one of their members quaintly put it. Every landing was a blind challenge in a large cloud of dust from rotor action, the engineer opening all covers and cleaning the filters the minute the engine was shut down. However, their twenty-four seater Mi1 Mi-8 Hip, the holder of several heavy-duty world records, was an ideal work-horse for the job, its gas turbine engines mounted above the cabin which was free at the centre of gravity to accommodate a large payload. On each sortie the helicopter was loaded with powdered milk for children or medical teams and supplies that could not possibly arrive by road. Sometimes they would stop on the way, dropping off a doctor or Russian wheat for a small remote village en route. They were the first to see the long winding line of people all heading towards the drop zone, some of whom had travelled three or four days on foot, just to glean.

Luftwaffe Transall C·160 air-dropping at Meranya
Photo Dany Gignoux ICRC

Frequently the Polish helicopter would carry one of the Red Cross medical teams based at Addis, who would set up a small tent beside the DZ and work tirelessly throughout the day. On occasions two Polish helicopters could be seen beside the DZ, with a queue of up to 1,000 people waiting to be treated. After the last air drop, the crew helped the landing party load recovered sacks and equipment, lifting off with them as shadows lengthened and daylight faded into apricot sunset, tinting the long white caravan of loaded human backs as they bore their precious cargo on a several miles trudge to the feeding centre.

The Polish assistance was crucial to success. With it, air dropping began in earnest on February 13th when Colonel Pogorzelski flew the landing party up to Rabel, and two RAF captains, Wing Commander Nicolle and Flight Lieutenant Nigel Voute, skippered the first Hercules sortie over the drop zone to start what became the largest air-drop operation in the peacetime history of the RAF and of the Luftwaffe.

Right to the last there were frustrations. The first air-drop had in fact been planned for the previous day but there was a public parade in the city and suddenly all the bowser drivers at Lidetta were mustered and driven off to support it, leaving the Polish helicopters with no fuel (the cost of which was borne by the UN). However, eventual

success the next day was followed up by John Clements and a LXX crew continuing the good work at Rabel, his Hercules and a Transall gearing into the daily air-drop routine.

Air-dropping started at Meranya, south of Rabel, four days later, on February 17th. It was found to be fairly straightforward, on a noticeably less hairy plateau than that at Rabel. Keen to get things started, the Polish crew had set off before they were provisioned for the day. This was rectified by Hercules delivery – on the second drop of the day cheese sandwiches and a bottle of Scotch arrived in a harness pack by parachute – cementing Anglo-Polish relations which were already developing into a splendid rapport between Polish crews and air despatchers.

But there was another story behind the 'flying Red Label.' Concerned that aircraft could be benighted on an airstrip for want of a small delicate part, Brian tasked the despatchers with producing suitable packaging which could be dropped under a small parachute and sustain shock – by day or after dark in the landing lights of the stranded aircraft. They looked at the traditional horsehair and foam padding and eventually came up with an apt solution – to pack the delicate item in grain!

"They promised me it would work", said a sceptical Brian. "So I told them to prove it by dropping a bottle of Red Label with a message to the Poles thanking them for their help and co-operation. I gather they had to be gently restrained from drinking it there and then!"

Needless to say, on his next visit to the Polish camp there was a gift of a bottle of vodka in return. Hot water for tea making and lunch was delivered daily onto the DZ by parachute in a harness pack.

As the rhythm of air-dropping settled, Bole Airport became a hive of labour-intensive load preparation. All relief grain in the Addis Ababa storehouses was reserved for air-dropping and conveyed to the airport in a continuous stream of lorries. Here it was split and double – sometimes triple – bagged into the stronger outer sacks on a large grass patch near detachment headquarters by tireless local labourers who carried it manually on their backs and heads to the assembly point between the two areas where the sacks were weighed, clustered on the pallets and tied. The proud badge of 47 AD, a golden Dakota in a blue sky (an honour awarded after the Battle of Arnhem in September 1944 when 116 despatchers lost their lives) mingled with the throng, weighing, tying, clipping, humping and pushing, driving forklifts, supervising and lashing down the loads with which they would fly. As each flight returned to take on more clustered loads, the pace intensified. Colonel Escheti, the extremely hard-working RRC co-ordinator, visited the detachment at least

Teaming up for mapping on an early drop zone recce. Staffan de Mistura (Food and Agriculture Organisation expert with the UN) with Polish and British air crews. Photo S. de Mistura, UN

twice a day, very early to see off the first flight and then in the afternoon to the 'Ops' tent for a hob-nob with the detachment commander and a joint decision on arrangements for the next day's deliveries. With a somewhat formal dignity, there was a double handshake on agreement of each plan. But nevertheless, he was a friendly and likeable man, a great ally to the aviators.

One Hercules was assigned to air-dropping while the second continued the air-landing operation, delivering grain from Assab. The Luftwaffe allotted one of their two Transalls solely for air dropping, flying it up to Addis from Dire Dawa daily. They had learnt rapidly and well the lessons from earlier problems and were dropping with a fair degree of accuracy, depending much more on the angle of the aircraft, whereas the British success was a combination of eye, mind and sheer push.

Throughout February and March air-dropping continued at Rabel, Meranya and two other drop zones, at Bure Mudaito and Gundo Meskel, which had not been reached by road transport for over a year. Each new operation was preceded with a previous day's visit by helicopter, a Bell 206B JetRanger provided by Helimission, the Swiss based relief agency, for survey and mapping. This was frequently a Chinese puzzle, for some of the villages had a habit of moving (either for grazing or because they were washed out or starved out, or for military or other reasons), the RRC officials were using maps produced in a survey over forty years ago, and the Swiss pilot was using yet another map! Consequently the RAF pilot in the survey party had to photograph the DZ and its approaches, his sketch map including all recognisable landmarks. The altitude of nearly all the drop zones (some even higher than those used in Nepal), made every flight performance critical. In addition to his detachment commander's duties, Brian Nicolle made a point of flying an air drop sortie every other day. As new crews arrived, they were screened over each DZ by him or another experienced captain.

In the early days there were some close calls, especially when a pilot was trying to cope for the first time with an air-drop approach at twenty-five feet along downward sloping ground. If the speed/power/height was not just right there was always the risk of putting the aircraft in a stall configuration at the end of the drop. Once or twice it nearly happened. There was more than one involuntary touch-down, and several tree strikes, taking the tops off trees near either end of the DZ. A number of trees were cut down by local people when they realised the dangers.

Building a cluster. In the foreground are the roller conveyors from the aircraft floor which convey the clusters to the edge of the ramp.
Photo by Dany Gignoux ICRC

The DZ at Bure Mudaito had a surface of flat baked sand in a 3,517-feet-high 'valley' surrounded by mountains. North-east of Addis, it was near a politically sensitive area east of the Awash river and it had to be reached in a round-about way on a seventy-three miles track almost due east and then a northerly heading for the last fifty-two miles, not only to avoid overflying the prohibited region but also to keep a respectful distance from the high ridged Ayelu mountain, frequently covered in cloud. But it was an interesting VFR flight, with the lakes and river valleys below attractive checkpoints. Here, Flight Lieutenants Ed Coleman and Dave Molyneux and crew delivered the millionth pound of air-dropped grain on the last day of February. On March 20th the three millionth pound of grain was despatched by the same crew on Rabel DZ. There was an extra celebratory harness pack containing French champagne. Over the radio the Polish crew was toasted: "Letenacy" ("your health"), by Sergeant Bob Szafran, a Polish-speaking air despatcher! The salutations were returned as the Helimission Bell 206B JetRanger filled the air with the whirr of its blades, piloted by Colonel Tsegaye Wolde, vice-president of the central committee of the RRC, bringing UN co-ordinator Kurt Jansson to assess progress. On March 30th the four millionth pound of grain was despatched at Bure Mudaito.

Gundo Meskel, 76 miles due north of Addis Ababa, was a 600 yards long DZ on a high plateau with a south-westerly approach. It had a good surface of parched grass and, apart from its 8,202 feet altitude, it afforded few problems on a westerly run-in.

* * *

Cost of the British operation went up by a half to £1.5 million a month as air-dropping got underway, shared between defence and overseas administration. The initial order of sacks was paid for by a firm in Wales – the standard service sack of triple jute, and in limited supply. The nylon ballistic sacks, made by Remploy, were also in short supply and other outlets were explored. They looked at sandbags, but vetoed them because of the arsenic in the material.

Once more Lyneham became the busy source of supply, packing each Hercules until it was bursting at the seams with sacks and pallets. But this time it was the 'little Army' down the road which was given the financial authority by the MoD to equip the air-drop operation with a constant stock of sacks, baseboards and lashings. It was a big military commitment for such a small squadron. Its quartermaster, Major Alan Batty, was totally responsible for acquiring 60,000 sacks and 504 baseboard pallets each week as well as cordage and other necessities. His main problem was predetermining quantities as the duration of the operation was unknown and extended a month at a time.

"The first call came on a Friday – for a deployment on Monday. I could not get hold of MoD for financial authority. Bridport Aviation, who were supplying the internal sacks and cordage contacted Save the Children, who offered an immediate contribution. Another headache was getting the stockpiles into Addis Ababa – cargo space in aircraft is limited and shipping from Cyprus would have been better. But it was not to be", he recalled.

Waiting for treatment from a clinic in one of two Polish relief helicopters beside the DZ.
Photo Dany Gignoux

The pallets, made in the UK to a very high specification for NATO operations, were of fine quality but expensive, costing £30.10 each board. The Royal Electrical and Mechanical Engineers 48 Cyprus workshop at Akrotiri, became aware that a composite board of hardwood, sawdust and resin, made on the island by Cypriot manufacturers, could be produced in Cyprus at a much cheaper rate. So it was bought in the local markets and taken to the REME workshop where local employees cut it to size and drilled holes in the right places, six pallets at a time. The forty-one civilian workers, carpenters and metal smiths, worked by rotation, four in a team. Each pallet weighed fifty pounds and cost about £12. It was a saving of nearly £400,000 by the end of the year.

Warrant Officer II Mike Ash, who masterminded the project from its inception said: "Few of the pallets were recoverable so we were confronted with the need for cheaper ways of producing them. If we had known that this was to go on for so long we may well have produced them even cheaper."

At the height of production the workshops produced 200 pallets a day which, from March onwards, were delivered to the cargo bay at RAF Akrotiri for overnight loading on the weekly supply Hercules or on special flights of VC10s and TriStars from RAF Brize Norton, already loaded with sacks.

Air Loadmaster Michael Coles checking pallet restraints after taking off from RAF Akrotiri.
Photo author

W/O Mike Ash inspects four Cypriot carpenters preparing pallets by drilling holes for cordage, at the REME workshop in Cyprus.
Photo author

Always on the lookout for economic improvements, at Lyneham Major Lewis had long been pondering on the shortcomings of the cordage (also very expensive) which secured the clusters and was expected to break at a predetermined force. It did not always oblige. Driving to base one morning he was held up behind a truck full of bricks covered in plastic.

"It set me thinking", he said. "We contacted the Swindon makers of the plastic and the result was a constant supply of plastic heatshrink covers from May onwards. It was much more effective in keeping the clusters together and in stopping the grain from moving in turbulence, thereby avoiding incidences of jamming in the aircraft. It was also much quicker to pack, with a nice shiny surface and things did not get caught up in it."

The cover reduced the amount of cordage needed and stopped the grain from 'settling' and the braided nylon cord from stretching when loaded overnight. To reduce weight in the aircraft the standard heavy conveyor rollers were changed for lighter equipment.

For the air despatchers themselves a month of pushing a total of 1,600 pounds at a time and repeating the performance throughout the day was strenuous enough, let alone having to work at an altitude where air starvation was the biggest factor. Added to this, in the heat of the action, trying to ensure that a foot was not caught in the roller conveyor and keeping one's balance as the aircraft banked to steer clear of a mountain or hit a pocket of turbulence needed some concentration. One hapless despatcher tripped over the ramp with the load and found himself hanging, spinning madly on his monkey line in the wake of the aircraft. Although he was whipped back into the aircraft by his colleagues in seconds, it was a horrific experience. That they all stood up to their stint so well speaks much for their stamina and toughness.

In the light of new experiences there were a number of adjustments to heavy free-drop flying techniques. It was obvious that much of the success rate depended on the height from which the sacks were dropped – the lower the better rate of success. There was a fine dividing line between an acceptable distance from the ground and the ideal gravity force which, with the forward movement generated by the aircraft, turned the baseboard into an aerofoil with a single complete rotation, landing base first. Wherever possible the run-in was flown at twenty-five feet pulling up to thirty-five feet at the point of despatch. The loadmaster told the captain the floor angle needed – the right nose-high attitude aiding despatch. Nothing much could be done about speed. There were constant reminders to compare altimeters, of flap setting, landing gear and pressurisation checks (where, because of continual opening, there was a natural leakage).

It quickly became apparent that, such was the accuracy of despatch, subsequent drops after the first one were damaging grain bags already on the ground. It was also noticeable that the crowd congregated one side or the other on the slopes beside the DZs. Using his crews' competence to advantage Brian devised a plan whereby the first drop of the day was about ten yards to the side of the centre marker, followed by the second drop about five yards away, both on the side furthest away from the crowd. The remaining two runs, as the pilot got his 'eye' in, were five and ten yards nearer the crowd but still within the safety parameter.

"The accuracy was very good. The problem with these small DZs was the length of 'throw', not the sideways displacement", he said.

Then there were the idiosyncrasies of each individual DZ which, as one pilot, Flight Lieutenant Peter Harborne, put it with typical understatement, were "not impossibly difficult but could make you pay attention!" His own crew were to air-drop 1,254,000 pounds of food during one three-week detachment.

But the greatest change of all was in the political atmosphere. The RRC officials were reaching the drop-zones and doing sterling work in controlling supplies as they were delivered and taken to distribution centres. There was a great deal of co-operation from village elders who ruled some considerably large pockets of population with a somewhat primitive discipline. From the oldest to the youngest, staggering along in the queue with his single sack, there was one big heart to succeed. Now that the Ethiopian Government had proved to their own satisfaction that they could control supplies they believed in airdropping themselves.

CHAPTER TEN

'Tralls' and other Turbos

BY the start of 1985 over fifty relief aircraft were operating into the various airstrips, many on a daily basis. The great bulk of cargo was carried by Lockheed's heavy freighter, the military C-130 or the L-100-30, designed for civilian cargo operation. Those operators who used other types of aircraft, with the best will in the world, were unable to produce the same logistics. The size of Ethiopia's grim tragedy without doubt imbued all aircrews with a spirit of competitiveness to deliver the most (and quickly) just to keep people alive. However, all did their level best. The big lifters fed the smaller light aircraft which transported supplies into regions inaccessible to the large turboprops, landing on tiny village strips or dirt roads. The heroic helicopter pilot taking a calculated risk to land a few sacks of food on some rocky outcrop, to meet the needs of a starving mountain hamlet – so remote that no live beast of burden could reach it – was just as much a vital part of the rescue package as the tough and efficient crews of the large multi-engined aircraft. The rugged twin turboprops operated by some of the European detachments, if not able to carry the same weight as the C-130, were quick on turn-round and eminently suitable for the short rocky strips to be found in

Ethiopia. However, the bulk of all heavy lifting was done by the RAF, the Red Cross in their chartered C-130s and the Luftwaffe with their Transall C-160s.

"I deplored comparison. The fact that there was an international contribution was good in itself. The aircraft differed vastly. They offered what they had and did what they could", said Derek Kingsman.

There was great Anglo-German co-operation. The squadrons were old friends with regular exchange pilots, in fact one West German pilot, Hauptmann Hans Muller, was to do his stint on Operation Bushel as captain of a Hercules crew before finishing his three years exchange tour with 30 Squadron.

Based at Dire Dawa the ungainly 'Tralls', as they were fondly known by their Luftwaffe crews, not only flew the regular grain lifts from Assab to Asmara, Axum, Makalle, Alamata, Gondar and Metemma. They also delivered where famine had emerged fifty miles to the south and

Unloading medical supplies from a Luftwaffe Transall C-160 at Axum during an early flying programme lifting grain and supplies from the port of Massawa. Photo West German Luftwaffe

east of the capital, to Lalibella and the short strips at Dessie and Behar Dar, from sunrise to sunset on at least three missions a day. Until February, when one aircraft was reserved for air-dropping, the two, in a continuous operation, carried 14,676 tonnes of relief goods from the Red Sea harbours. For five months two more, sometimes three, were on relief work in the Sudan. The base at Dire Dawa was used as a maintenance centre for all technical repairs necessary on the West German Government's whole Africa contribution. Old hands in Ethiopia, they had flown helicopters on relief missions in the famine of 1974.

The airfield at Dire Dawa had good facilities, a 9,000 feet concrete runway with NDB and VOR, navaids and fairly efficient air traffic control. It was shared with a small detachment from the German Democratic Republic flying Soviet manufactured aircraft – three Ilyushins, Il-76T or Il-86s and an An-20 and An-26 and operating a split detachment at Dire Dawa and Assab; Aeroflot An-12s, partly based at Addis, and Hip helicopters, Ethiopian Airlines DC-3s and a C-130 of the Italian Air Force, most on some degree of famine relief. Although this was designated an international civilian airport, there was a strong Ethiopian military presence and some 3,000 Russian and Cuban troops, the latter the remnants of an 18,000 strong fighting force sent in during the late 1970s to support Ethiopia in the Ogaden war, and now keeping watch on the uneasy Somalia-Ethiopia border.

The Luftwaffe crews, soon to become familiar sights in their bright orange flying suits, were rotated with their aircraft every three weeks. At the end of 1984, when it became obvious that the operation was going to be prolonged, the Air Transport Wing decided to divide the task between LTG.61, 62 and 63. Their Franco-German seventy-six tonnes Transall C-160s, powered by Rolls-Royce Tynes and able to carry up to 37,500 pounds, were identifiable by their badges, a bee or a goat, denoting that they were from transport units LTG.63 at Hohn, north of Hamburg, or LTG.61 at Landsberg, near Munich respectively, or a blind crow if hailing from the LTG.62 FFS-S Instrument Flying School at Wunstorf near Hanover. They were not equipped for passengers but each load in Ethiopian conditions averaged about thirteen tonnes.

Like the British they were highly motivated by the plight and misery of the people and found the flying challenging and adventurous. A new departure for them was finding themselves in the same aviation environment as their East German cousins with whom, after a wary and somewhat formal beginning, they built up some rapport. It soon became obvious that their various East Bloc

Transall navigator Oberleutnant Norbert Berg hands out a gift of tinned food to a hungry Ethiopian family at Lallibella.
Photo West German Luftwaffe

neighbours brought in more arms than grain. As they assisted in loading and unloading the West German aircraft the local people would whisper: "We want food, not guns."

Needless to say they experienced the day-to-day vicissitudes, burst tyres, stone damage, sand and dust ingestion, birdstrikes (a bad confrontation with a vulture caused extensive damage, not only puncturing the Transall cockpit but bouncing off onto the wing leading edge and destroying internal wiring), and the joys of an engine change in 30° C during the first ten days of operation.

The first detachment commander, Hohn-based LTG.63 Oberstleutnant Jo Schuller, started an early flying programme of lifting grain from Assab to Asmara and Axum where, on the short airstrip, they had a hairsbreadth near miss with a donkey and, on another day, with a camel, all surviving with only the loss of dignity. This was not an easy strip at the best of times: there were constant warnings from Transamerica crews of the risk of missiles aimed by trigger-happy guerillas.

Anxious to assess the conditions under which the Transalls had to operate (far beyond the bounds of normal military standards in Europe or anywhere else in the world), Jo Schuller took on much of the early flying, initiating younger and less experienced pilots and telling them that they had to learn to fly all over again – without

Offloading in 'Indian' country. Transall C·160 beside the short strip at Lallibella.
Photo West German Luftwaffe

much help from the manuals! On one of his first assignments he was persuaded by Paul Keller, a German International Red Cross representative, to airlift a Land Rover urgently needed by the Ethiopian Red Cross and ten tonnes of oil and other goods to Massawa's short strip beside the Red Sea, universally avoided by most operators as it was 'built' on the sand. Keller had taken the precaution to have the strip rolled by a two-ton roller but even so, with some misgivings Schuller took off from the near 8,000 feet high Asmara airport to cautiously overfly the strip while considering the odds of becoming bogged down; but he eventually landed with no problems in the steamy, sandy, sea level atmosphere.

By November 27th each 'Trall' had completed 160 and 305 flying hours in the field, conveying the large bulk of food and medical supplies donated by West Germany and wheat from Australia, Canada and the USA. At Lalibella, where they were to deliver a large amount of food and medical supplies, the gravel runway had a much-used footpath across it, very near the town. Here the poor harvest the year before had been almost completely destroyed by pests and 8,000 people were starving, with up to fifty dying daily. Unlike the British detachment which, with their larger aeroplanes, had at first been able only to contact people on the major strips, more remote from the centres of population, the full horror of the famine was to strike them on their first landing. They had hardly stopped when the aircraft was surrounded by masses of gaunt people in rags. When the loadmaster,

Two-storey tokuls near Lalibella.
Photo Ethiopian Airlines

Hauptfeldwebel Schimanski opened the ramp and door he found an old, skeletal man standing naked before him. He was so shocked that he jumped back into the hold and grabbed his own 'civvies', thrusting the clothing at the old man who turned with his precious gift to force his way through the crowd and promptly had it torn from him. He was left standing hopeless and crying. The navigator Oberleutnent Norbert Berg, called a few women and children forward and the crew handed out their own rations, protecting them as they ate. In the 12th and 13th centuries this small ancient city was designated by its devout people a second Jerusalem!

But the main problem with Lalibella was that it was in 'Indian country' and apt to change hands at short notice. On some of the smaller strips there was little control and the people fought, sometimes with sticks, to grab for themselves some wheat, cooking oil, blankets, tents or medical supplies. It became a habit at base for the crews to collect, before first take-off, bread, biscuits, anything edible, to give to hungry villagers.

*   *   *

In the neighbouring Red Sea republic of Djibouti, France based 3,250 servicemen at the request of the Djibouti government. The Force Aerienne de Djibouti comprised about six aircraft, most of them small, but intermittently a French Air Force Transall was based there to carry grain from the port to several of the smaller strips used regularly by the Germans, and also a Hercules to support Médecin Sans Frontières until the relief agency was banished by the Ethiopian Government for daring to criticise the southern resettlement programme and alleging that 100,000 people had died. France provided twenty-three per cent of EEC food relief and was also working on the obsolete rail link to Addis Ababa.

The French crews tended to operate with Gallic individuality, and one captain, Lt Bruno Constantin was well known as an extrovert by the Lyneham squadrons, where he had once been on an exchange posting with 47 Squadron.

Bruno breezed into Addis one day in his Transall, quite out of the blue, parked outside the detachment tents and demanded a load of grain. Space was very cramped and there were times when an aircraft had to stay in the hold while another took off. Always willing to reward enthusiasm Brian Nicolle arranged for Bruno's Transall to be loaded. However, he looked out some time later to find no sign of Bruno or his crew and the aircraft closed down. Sometime later Bruno appeared. Brian grabbed him and asked him why he had left the aircraft completely blocking the loading area.

"He looked at me with hurt surprise, shrugged and said 'Ze French lunch!'. He got a French and English reply!", Brian recalled.

There was, however, great admiration for Bruno when he talked himself, his crew and his aircraft out of an extremely tricky situation.

It happened on his last relief flight before returning home to France. On the approach to Lalibella with a load of grain he noticed that the area seemed quiet but that the few people to be seen were waving at him – and that there were some odd puffs of smoke around the strip. However, he landed and found the airfield deserted. Then someone appeared and told him that the airfield was in the hands of Tigrean rebels. It was impossible to take off on the short runway without at least partly off-loading and this he and his crew proceeded to do, out of range with the outside world and feeling distinctly uncomfortable. Halfway through, a party of armed rebels arrived and surrounded them.

At first they threatened to blow up the aeroplane but Bruno managed to talk them out of it saying that it was a mercy mission aircraft and that they would be highly unpopular with both the local people and the world at large. They then proceeded to question the crew, and most terrified of all was the Ethiopian Government 'minder', who feared that his hour had come. However, Bruno explained him away as his batman.

Eventually they were taken on a five hours march to a temporary rebel stronghold in the hills. Bruno did some very fast and clever talking, telling them that they would not be well thought of if the crew were harmed. He said that the highest rebel leaders would not be at all pleased and insisted that the local contingent contact the hierarchy. The result was an order for their immediate release and they were marched back to the airfield, arriving before daybreak two days later. Bruno took off just after dawn and made straight for Addis Ababa, arriving with his exhausted, dishevilled and unshaven crew just as the detachment was coming to life, and diving into 'HQ' to telephone the French Air Attaché.

The Italian Air Force deployed two of its fleet of twelve Aeritalia G.222 military transports at Asmara from November 12th, 1984 to March 18th, 1985, taking on grain from Massawa and delivering it to Makalle and Axum on a regular basis during the four and a half

Everything that made flying difficult made the light aircraft indispensible. Twin Otter flown by a Mission Aviation Fellowship pilot in the Ethiopian highlands. Photo MAF

months. Similar in design to the Franco-German Transall and powered by the same Rolls-Royce Tyne RTy 20 turboprops, the G.222 has considerably less capacity, with a maximum payload of 15,430 pounds, just over half of the Transall maximum. Nevertheless it made a small but significant contribution to relief in the beleaguered north. The aircraft were rotated and, including deliveries direct from Italy, carried 7,074,896 pounds of food and medical supplies given by the Italian government, and conveyed over 400 passengers, flying over 773 hours in the field.

Italian Air Force C-130s and a Transamerica L-100-30 chartered by the Government delivered 2,188,541 pounds of food and medicines donated by Italy to Asmara and Addis Ababa, transporting over 300 relief workers from Italy and flying 545 hours on Ethiopian relief missions.

*   *   *

Of all light aeroplanes used in Ethiopian relief two types of turboprop aircraft, the de Havilland Canada Twin Otter and the single-engined Pilatus PC-6 Turbo-Porter, made

An aeriel survey
by Twin Otter
of the feeding
camps at
Makalle.
Photo
Dany Gignoux

the most impact on the famine. With their excellent short take-off and landing (STOL) capabilities they seemed to revel in mountain flying and the short and stony strips which had traditionally been considered suitable only for small piston engined singles.

It was one ball game flying a large stolid Hercules or Transall over the mountainous territory with its accompanying turbulence and vertical air currents, non-existent horizons and even optical illusions, but quite another flying light aircraft in these conditions and landing on strips which were but a miniature of the larger airstrips and some of the dropping zones. A number of tiny airstrips were on top of mountain ridges or on a flat platform half way down a mountain with one side an awful sheer drop, the other a cliff with side clearance less than twelve feet from the wing tip. There could be a seemingly bottomless gorge at one end (or both), a situation which almost every pilot on relief flying in the Ethiopian highlands encountered. The easier strips were but a flat piece of ground. Small airstrips could change from

PC-6 Pilatus Turbo-Porter on the airstrip at Meychou after delivering a load of supplies.
Photo Dany Gignoux

friendly to enemy hands in between flights and each had to be scanned to see what was going on below, and to look for straying people or animals. Each landing could be a battle against up draughts or down draughts. Because of the mountains the aircraft were frequently out of radio range. The wet season was a major factor, with flying in tension conditions up to six months of the year. Strong winds could threaten to throw a light aircraft against a ragged mountain spur just off the wing tip. A violent dust storm (the dreaded haboob) could pulp a fragile aluminium aeroplane as if it was balsa wood.

But everything that made flying difficult made the small aeroplanes indispensable. A ten minute flight could equal more than a day's travel on the ground. As a flying ambulance, a task the pilots were frequently to perform, there was a short and comfortable ride to hospital as against the questionably survivable hell of several days bumping in the heat and dust over mountains tracks. They were a lifeline to so many small towns and settlements which needed help but did not have an airstrip that could handle a large freighter.

Until the heavy transports arrived, some of the feeding centres had totally relied on the small aircraft to bring in food – a hopeless losing battle against starvation spurred on only by the defiant scream of human need. Now, as the large air freighters disgorged their bulk cargoes at Makalle and other centres of distribution the light aircraft took on another dimension which, until air-dropping got under way, was a crucial link in the chain of relief – the onward transportation of food to the hungry hinterland villages. For only about twenty per cent of the affected areas had airstrips suitable to handle the big lifters.

The light aeroplanes provided transport for the last twenty-five, fifty or 100 miles, a life-link which became a familiar sight in a corner of the larger airstrips at Makalle, Gondar and Axum, and later the small strips beside the drop zones, taking on food from the EEC, Canada, Live Aid or Band Aid and numerous other relief charities as it left the cargo bay of a Hercules.

The Twin Otter, a twenty-seater with a maximum payload of 4,280 pounds, a non-retractable tricycle landing gear and optional cargo doors, was a far more practical proposition for humping supplies to remote deprived areas than the valiant small aeroplanes and their altruistic aviators who had selflessly undertaken the task since the end of World War II. Needing a take-off run of only 700 feet and a landing run of 515 feet, it has alternative high flotation wheels and tyres which were used for soft field conditions during the rainy season. It is even capable of being armed, an advantage not lost to the Ethiopian Forces which bought three for the Army Air Corps as photo survey aircraft.

Until 1985 Ethiopian Airlines, which has an extensive if intermittent internal network serving forty centres of population, had relied on an aging fleet of Gooney Birds. Impressed with the Twin Otters' performance in the field, the airline started a replacement programme of some of the DC-3s, purchasing five Twin Otters from de Havilland Canada for the network, and a sixth for aerial survey with a grant from the Canadian Export Development Corporation.

World Vision, the international relief agency, first placed a Twin Otter in Ethiopia in 1981 and were eventually to use two to serve their eight relief camps throughout the country. In fact, one of their aircraft, crewed by Mission Aviation Fellowship pilots, flew to Alamata and Korem the BBC television team whose film in 1984 alerted the world (*see Chapter 15*).

The versatile little Pilatus PC-6 Turbo-Porter, equipped with a Pratt and Whitney PT6A-27 turbine engine, was to become the busy aerial mini-moke of the relief programme. Four Porters, five pilots (one on standby) and a small maintenance crew were contracted by the International League of the Red Cross from Swiss-based Zimex Aviation, an airline vastly experienced in international aid, which had worked for the ICRC since 1980. The airline's remaining ten Porters and five Twin Otters were actively engaged in African relief, and it was also operating an aerial control programme of cassava pests with a Volpar Turbo Beech 18.

The four Red Cross Porters, proudly displaying the insignia on the fuselage and a smaller White Cross of Switzerland on their tails, had dual bases – at Asmara and Makalle. Asmara was used as a maintenance base where one aircraft was located and used mainly for passengers until one of the Makalle-based aircraft was due for maintenance, when they were exchanged. From Makalle the Porters transported up to their maximum of just over one tonne of Red Cross supplies into thirty-six wild and woolly airstrips of which all but eight had 'nil facilities' in the true sense of the word! However, the pilot had a wide field of vision through the large sliding side doors which could be opened and closed in flight and, with the aircraft's low stalling speed of forty-four knots, time and care could be taken to weigh up the options below. One Pilatus Turbo-Porter load could provide basic rations for sixty people for one month. Up to 660 pounds of supplies could be dropped through the floor hatch which could also be opened and closed by the pilot without assistance. It was tailor-made for deliver-and-get-the-hell-out-of-it sorties.

Its STOL capabilities were superb: it could take off fully loaded in 400 feet, with a landing roll of 375 feet. With wing tanks fitted, it had a range of over 700 miles and was fitted with an engine air inlet when used in dusty desert conditions. During the crisis months each aircraft flew 140 hours per month making seven flights a day, to the physical limits of each pilot, with an accident-free record until early in November 1985. Then one aircraft overshot the bumpy, tricky 800 feet runway (a one-way only approach over a mountain ridge just 200 yards away, irrespective of wind direction) at Meychou, and went into a ditch. It was transported back to Zürich with its sore nose by a home-going Belgian Air Force Hercules.

During 1985 the four Porters (later reduced to three) flew 822 days (3,700 hours) making 7,414 landings, many on makeshift airstrips too rough for the Twin Otter. Between them the aircraft transported 2,789 tonnes of relief cargo for the Red Cross, most of it flown one-way, and 12,000 passengers.

* * *

Meanwhile at Bole on one side the British and Belgian detachments and on the other the Soviets continued to observe each other's comings and goings and occupations with quiet interest, separated by 200 yards of dispersal area. The Russians were joined on their side of the commercial area by three Libyan-operated An-26s, even more of a menace in the skies than the Soviets for they had obviously never flown to quadrantal rules and were liable to be met head-on. They seemed to sit on the ground most of the time and it was rumoured that they were told by the Ethiopian authorities to get on with the job or go. They did move some supplies but did not stay long. Occasionally an enormous Soviet-operated An-22 Cock would spread-eagle itself over the pan while it disgorged a Mil Mi-24 Hind helicopter – an impressive sight.

But there were signs that the ice was melting. One day a Russian Air Force officer managed a cheery wave at the occupants of a departing RAF crew bus. This was shortly followed by not one, but three invitations to visit the An-12s – a rare concession indeed! Then in April, to everyone's surprise, the An-12s restarted moving some grain, a token gesture which involved borrowing RAF forklifts and flatbeds! It had been remarked that their natural habitat appeared to be more on the airfield than in the air.

CHAPTER ELEVEN

Red Cross and Mission Hercules

AVIATION aid from the West soon evolved into each military or civilian operator working his own patch, though frequently on the loading bay together at Assab and again at airfields in areas of highest distribution. All C-130 operations, apart from the RAF, were eventually based at Asmara, where frequently as many as six C-130s, military and civilian, could be seen on line at night, together with Italian G.222s and East Bloc aircraft including a strong contingent of gun-turreted An-12s. There was a military area and a civilian area on opposite sides of the runway, and a large contingent of Ilyushin Il-30 May reconnaisance aircraft. Quaintly, the armed Soviets parked themselves among the civilians. Perhaps they felt safer from the over-enthusiastic Ethiopian Army tank commanders, frequently heard in action in the military area. The airfield had been heavily fortified after an attack by guerillas in early 1984 when some aircraft were damaged.

Most of the Western air and ground crews were billeted nearby in the idyllic old town with its wide cool boulevards and Roman architecture, shaded by bougainvillaea and jacaranda – hauntingly reminiscent of its Italian colonisers and ancient African kingdoms. But accommodation was at a premium and, as at Addis, the strict curfew limited operations.

At the height of the emergency, operators from nine nations were supplying aircraft to aid famine relief, a number of them chartered by the International Committee of the Red Cross and its subsidiaries, the League of Red Cross and Red Crescent Societies and the Ethiopian Red Cross Society. Four Hercules operators, Transamerica, Air Botswana and the Belgian and Swedish Air Forces, were directly chartered to the ICRC which, under the Geneva Convention, had a mandate to fly relief supplies into anti-government areas not catered for by the RRC. Because of this it controlled its own supplies and distributed them to its own nine feeding centres either by charter or using its own transport. The Red Cross had been battling drought in Ethiopia for many years, and the C-130 charter crews were no strangers to flying in extremely difficult and complicated conditions, one day in the comparative calm of Government-held country, the next in rebel-held areas or the no-man's-land of disputed

territory. About half of the cargo was trucked by road or rail, a comparatively short journey from the Red Sea port of Massawa, though some grain was loaded at the somewhat primitive 6,200 feet long gravel and sand airstrip near the port. However, it was highly unpopular because of the strong concentration of salt which had a detrimental corrosive effect on the aircraft, and the Red Cross were advised that it would be used only in an emergency. The other half was lifted at Assab.

Transamerica Airlines' operations were greatly admired by RAF crews. Some felt that, while the RAF had the credit for being 'first' (the British rescue mission was of course the first Government-sponsored military operation to arrive), the Transamerica L-100-30 crews had been the real pioneers, whose brains had been avidly picked and advice eagerly sought by the Brits before flying into the unknown. Then members of a large and active charter airline, the tough, laconic American crews were no strangers to trouble spots and had been operating two, three and sometimes four aircraft for the International Red Cross and other relief agencies in Ethiopia since June 1984. Despite the obvious disadvantages of flying 'stretched' C-130s into the terrain, they had been the first to land where formerly only Ethiopian Airlines Dakotas were the largest aircraft to be seen. They had just about everything thrown at them, from rebel missiles aimed in flight to two tyre bursts on the same side during

A C-130 Hercules of the 15th Wing Transport and Communications Command, Belgian Air Force, flying over Ethiopia.
Photo Karel Vervoort, Belgian Air Force

a landing at Makalle. They had initiated a Red Cross briefing for crews and established great rapport with all the other C-130 operators, including the RAF. Nothing was too much trouble, if they could help.

At first based at Addis Ababa, Transamerica moved their headquarters to Asmara at the end of October 1984. The big cargo bay of their 'Super Hercules' was much envied by Mk 1 operators. The freight cabin volume was extended by a double fuselage plug of fifteen feet, enabling it to carry the same standardised pallets as a Boeing 747 freighter. Stripped of all frills and military accessories, without the usual 'passage' for airmovers, it was filled to the hilt. At times it seemed as if the distinctive blue-green tails with the trellised T were everywhere, loading and unloading, taking on fuel, turning round, flying in, flying out. They shifted their large loads like lightning, with very few handlers.

The Belgian Air Force threw itself wholeheartedly into the famine relief effort in Africa. At changeover times half its fleet of twelve C-130H aircraft could be found in various parts of the Continent and in fact at the height of the crisis more than half its Hercules hours were flown over Africa. At first two aeroplanes and two crews were detached on Red Cross deliveries in Ethiopia (another was already operating in Zaire and later in the year the BAF was to initiate an airbridge in the Sudan).

The first two aircraft, from the 15th Wing Transport and Communications Command based at Melsbroek, Brussels, flew into Addis Ababa on December 19th 1984 under the command of Melsbroek's station commander Colonel Karel Vervoort, who was to take a very active part in relief flying. One of his most vivid memories of that period was the sight of two Belgian and two RAF Hercules sitting on the loading ramp at Bole, their leading edges packed with birds.

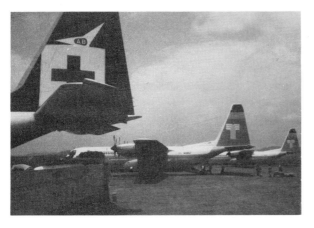

"There they were, happily chatting, as the crews arrived to start their working day. On the other side of the ramp, on the contrary, several Antonov 12s did not host a single bird! It was obvious that even the birds knew which aircraft were transporting food."

Although Bole Airport was considered the safest base for the Hercules fleets they could not all be handled on the limited parking area. Another major problem was the availability of fuel which the RAF were also facing, with airport authorities decreeing that commercial airlines should have priority, an impasse which was solved with some diplomacy. Most of the relief operators, including the British detachment, kept going by uplifting fuel at Assab, where there was normally no shortage, while loading.

The Belgian contingent transferred to Asmara in April, where they were to set up a base for one Hercules on regular Red Cross deliveries. Here the fuel situation was no better. Sometimes it was cut off without notice because, apparently, the powers that be set other priorities. Arbitrarily the Ethiopian military authorities would warn the relief flyers that fuel would not be available for the next five or six days. Not to be thwarted, they would operate the first flight of the day into Makalle and then onto Assab where both fuel and freight were available, continuing Makalle-Assab operations throughout the day and returning to Asmara with enough fuel for the first Makalle-Assab flight next day. Fortunately this situation was short-term.

One of the most interesting aspects of the whole airlift was how each operator met universal problems of terrain and altitude, and some singular ones of their own and how they coped individually, often with different solutions. Blown tyres on the rockstone surfaces of runways at Makalle, Axum and Gondar were a constant headache for the Belgians.

"As long as the tyre deflated slowly it was relatively easy to get the crocodile jack under its socket and simply replace the main wheel. But if the tyre exploded it usually damaged the main wheel well interior and doors", said Colonel Vervoort.

They also found that compressor seals and even blades could be completely eroded by sand and stones, and at one time fifteen engineers in the Sabena workshops 'next door' to the military base at Melsbroek were detailed to

Triple line-up at Makalle. Two Transamerica Airlines and an Air Botswana L-100-30 'stretched' Hercules after delivery. Photo Air Botswana

apply a special coating to seal off compressors. Another early problem was 'de-flouring' the aircraft on its return to Brussels, where even toothbrushes were used to get the wheat flour out of electronic and avionic equipment. This was solved by having a large military tent, handmade and tailored to aircraft dimensions, installed in the cargo hold with its opening facing aft on the loading ramp.

The Belgians ran a tight ship, the BAF aircrew of five assisting the four ground mechanics, even helping with repairs. They had a remarkably good turnover with never more than thirty personnel and high aircraft service-ability. During the peak crisis months each aircraft flew up to seven shuttles a day, bringing in about twenty tonnes on each flight. Deliveries from European charities in another aircraft included two for Abos, one for RTBF/ Communauté Français and another for Médicin Sans Frontières.

Some of the Belgian Hercules are equipped with VLA-GES (Very Low Altitude Gravity Extraction System), a sophisticated automatic despatch system for air-dropping which permits air drops of twelve to sixteen tonnes in one single run with a high success rate, burst sacks number-ing about two per cent. It relies on the best compromise between gravity and weight, the vertical (accelerating) speed and horizontal speed of the load on impact. Like the German system, it needs a positive pitch up of the floor at the drop point.

Needless to say the BAF were eager to use their re-sources and start air-dropping, with hopes of specialising in this method of delivery, but as Karel Vervoort put it: "It took a hell of a long time before we were officially allowed to air-drop relief supplies." They ran into the same red tape and suspicions as did the RAF and the Luftwaffe in obtaining diplomatic clearance.

Very occasionally the mercy flights would be con-fronted with unpleasant behaviour by an East Bloc crew. The Belgians had two incidents of intimidation at Makalle by Russian helicopters which hovered above each wing tip of their Hercules, blowing sand and stones into the fuselage with their rotor downwash and presenting a very real collision danger.

"It took a diplomatic complaint by our ambassador in Addis to stop the 'braveries'", commented Karel Vervoort wryly.

* * *

The Swedish Air Force was an experienced C-130 carrier for the Red Cross. Sweden maintained a strongly armed neutrality between East and West, with about 400 home-produced and Western military aircraft. The philanthropic Swedes had been participants in numerous short mercy operations for the Red Cross and the UN – in Africa, Asia and the Middle East – mostly with rescue equipment. During 1984 single flights had been made to Ethiopia for the Swedish and Finnish Red Cross with medical supplies, and a couple more were made early in 1985 for the Pentecostal Church and Lutheran Mission. In January the Red Cross requested the hire of a Hercules and crew for an initial ten weeks operation from March 11th to May 10th, delivering grain from the Red Sea ports to the Ethiopian feeding centres.

Lieutenant Colonel Ake Sveden, commander of the Air Transport Wing said: "Operation Bushel was in full swing and we were given some useful information through our Air Attaché in London. Compared with the resources of the RAF ours are small and the damage to aircraft and the rate of tyre bursts alarming to us."

The Swedish Air Force was in fact the first European air force to buy C-130s, and possessed eight. Because of the damage risks involved they decided to allocate an old faithful, SE-842, one of two purchased in the '60s with SE-843 remaining in Sweden as a back-up (their first buy, SE-841 was vetoed as underpowered for the high-level take-offs and landings as it still operated with the original A-7 engines). All three had been regularly used on Red Cross charters.

Preparation was extremely thorough, with useful techniques for keeping the single Hercules airworthy. The aeroplane had about fifteen antennae under the belly. Some were removed, and the remaining aerials and belly fully cladded. The flight deck and electronics were also protected from flour dust. Senior pilots were charged with finding new take-off and landing techniques to minimise the damage by stones from wheel rotation during the ground roll at Makalle, Axum and other gravel strips. This comprised lifting the nosewheel off the ground as early as possible during take-off roll and keeping it up for most of the landing run including the reverse thrust stage, with flaps at 20 degrees until the nose was lowered.

Loading Red Cross supplies trucked from Massawa to Asmara. Photo Dany Gignoux ICRC

They also devised an on-off system of reverse thrust to minimise dust ingestion in the engine intakes and other systems – when the dust reached the trailing edge of the wing as the aircraft slowed down, thrust was interrupted until the cloud was left behind and then continued. The crews also had a unique method of cleaning the cargo compartment after each flight. A rubber pipe was con-

A tight fit. Loading a Volvo truck into the Swedish Air Force Hercules. Photo Dany Gignoux ICRC

nected to an air valve in the hull and they then climbed to 15,000 feet to pressurise the aircraft.

"The pressure difference in the inside of the aircraft gave a good vacuum cleaning. In this way we managed to keep a clean aircraft, but polluted the countryside!" Lieutenant Colonel Sveden recalled.

Operation SWEALIE 1985 (The Swedish Air Force Air Lift in Ethiopia 1985) began on March 13th under the command of Major Uno Haglund, commander of the Air Transport Squadron, when the small contingent flew into Addis with sixteen tonnes of basing equipment and a large load of blankets for the Red Cross. Their first relief flight was made to Makalle the next day, continuing on to Assab for refuelling and a load of flour and beans. A week later they transferred to Asmara.

The Swedes ran an even tighter little ship than the Belgians, their small company of fifteen men consisting of two crews and a few technicians, changing every three weeks. They worked every day, one crew on an early shift and the second in the afternoon. One of the four pilots acted as detachment commander (Ake Sveden was to do his own three weeks stint as detachment commander and

pilot during the airlift). All flight engineers and load-masters in the Air Transport Wing came from a basic engineering background and so each contingent included up to nine people with the ability to maintain the aircraft, capable of engine changes if necessary and all systems repairs. The early crew started at 6.00 am when the airport opened with an overnight load and completed three shuttles during the morning. The second crew started in the early afternoon, having prepared a meal for the returning crew before taking over and flying two more lifts.

Battered but unbowed, the old Hercules stood up to the gruelling task like a champion, with just one engine shut down during flight because of low oil pressure. Throughout the whole period it flew every day with just one half day a week put aside for general maintenance. When the need for spares became vital to keep the operation going there were always the other friendly C-130 operators from whom to borrow or swap. In 267 flying

LANDING TECHNIQUE ON GRAVEL STRIPS

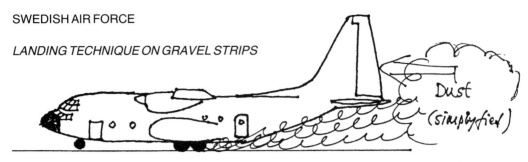

1 The pilot keeps the nosewheel in the air – orders "Flaps 20", which the co-pilot sets.

2 Smooth reverse with the nosewheel still out of ground (at speeds with effect on the rudder).

3 Nosewheel is lowered to the ground. The co-pilot sets "Flaps up". Steering with nosewheel.

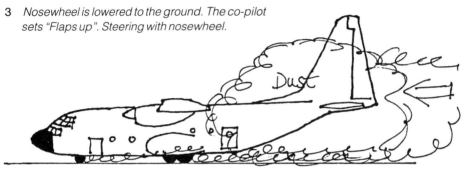

4 Reversing continued. Aft loadmaster positioned at paratroop-door and informs when the dustcloud reaches the trailing-edge of the wing. The reversing is then interrupted until the cloud is left behind. This procedure continues as long as necessary. Wheelbraking.

hours it delivered 3,550 tonnes of food and supplies, eventually returning to its base at Satenas for an extensive three weeks repair and cleaning. Such was the success of the Swedish Air Force mission that they were chartered again in August, when the wet season ended, for a further eighteen weeks.

The fourth Red Cross operator was Air Botswana Cargo with a L-100-30 (A2-ACA) which had been on charter to the International Red Cross since 1980 and a L-100-20 (A2-AEG), one of the earliest Hercules to be 'stretched' by Lockheed with a single plug fuselage extension of eight feet. The civil crews, like those of Transamerica, were vastly experienced in heavy bulk operations all over the world and equally quick on turnround. It was not unknown for them to load a twenty-one tonnes cargo of the standard fifty kilo bags of corn and tie it

down in eighteen minutes, off-loading the same cargo in fifteen minutes.

Air Botswana had lifted relief supplies into Asmara, Addis Ababa and Makalle as early as 1983 but it was not until September 1984 that regular Ethiopian airlifts started. At that time both aircraft were working for the Red Cross, alternating between Angola and Ethiopia. In December the Red Cross decided to concentrate the two aircraft in Angola until April 1985 when A2-ACA was transferred to Ethiopia, followed by A2-AEG a month later. This aeroplane was chartered for the Red Cross by Balair, a Swiss-based airline, as was a L-100-30 belonging to SF Air, a French cargo carrier experienced in international aid support. A2-AEG was then chartered to the Swedish-based Lutheran World Federation, a well organised collaboration between the Church of Sweden

Both ships at Axum.
Air Botswana's
L-100-20
and L-100-30.
Photo Air Botswana

Mission and Church of Sweden Aid/Lutherhjalpen for transportation and distribution.

Following the BAF move to Asmara A2-ACA was initially based at Bole where it became the first and only Hercules to fly into the 4,500 feet strip at Lalibella lifting fifteen tonnes three times a day.

"The strip has a quite spectacular approach and could only be negotiated by our crews with very positive flying and equally positive techniques during the take-off run! We were the only company to fly the Hercules into that field", Chas Hartridge, the Chief Flight Engineer proudly recalled.

He too paid tribute to the co-operation between the companies and military crews. "Airborne and ground co-operation – a real spirit between the crews. Spares were always readily lent to enable an operator to continue its mission."

The L-20 transferred to Asmara in May from where it started three or four schedules a day into Makalle and Axum. The two aeroplanes had singular operating differences, for whereas A2-ACA had a modern auxiliary power unit the older L-20 had the earlier gas turbine compressor which had some marked limitations at high airfields. Both were eventually based at Asmara, though occasional forays had to be made into Addis for a crew wash and brush up because of the limited living space in Asmara, already bursting at the seams with large numbers of airlift people. From Asmara they also lifted into Gondar and Barentu.

A tight schedule meant that maintenance had to be carried out during loading and unloading or at the end of the day before the 18.00 hours curfew. In the early days wheel changes were frequent but this decreased with reinforced tyres and a reduction in tyre pressure, and the improvements made to the impacted stone runways at Axum and Makalle, though not before quite severe under-body damage to both these 'stretched' aircraft. In addition leading-edge damage to the inboard undercarriage doors was a major problem and it was not unusual for doors to be replaced at least once in the period between base servicing. Experiments in handling techniques and improved aircraft protection brought damage down to a reasonable minimum.

Loads carried by both the aeroplanes varied from fifteen to twenty tonnes, depending on strip length, weather and temperature and fuel for the sector. Wheat flour, carried in quantities by all the operators, was the messiest and least popular cargo, invading every corner of the aircraft and its equipment. This was eventually restricted to the cargo bay by fitting a large plastic curtain between the flight deck and the hold. Butter oil was the most awkward as it came in large tin containers and took between thirty and forty-five minutes to load and once inside the freight bay, was difficult to restrain.

Over 500 flights completing 748 hours were flown for the Lutheran World Federation in 180 days, the bulk of them in A2-AEG, with some back up from the L-30. The two aircraft completed their missions at the end of February 1986, though in July A2-ACA was chartered by Caritas, the Catholic agency, for its own relief programme in Ethiopia.

Air Botswana's L-100-20 at Makalle. Under charter to the Lutheran World Federation.
Photo Tore Samuelsson

CHAPTER TWELVE

Human Cargo

AT first passengers were discouraged – 180 pounds of grain taking priority over 180 pounds of human weight and luggage. But in fact the RAF and the other international carriers were to transport many hundreds of people. Most carriers applied the criteria of need and benefit. There were circumstances where people were as vital to relief as the amount of supplies they displaced.

Health workers, doctors, nurses or sisters of the numerous religious orders and charities of all nationalities were, to many members of the British detachment, the earliest contacts with what was actually happening in the feeding centres and refugee settlements. As political suspicions were gradually allayed and trust and friendships built up, the benefit of allowing individual servicemen to visit the camps and clinics (always accompanied by their 'minder'!) became apparent to the authorities. The airmen saw at first hand the conditions under which their passengers worked and what they achieved. Wing Commander David Guest, one of eight detachment commanders who were to do their term, echoed the feelings of many when he said: "They are wonderful people who made us feel very humble. We were almost ashamed that we were enjoying ourselves."

So, without fuss or bureaucracy, whether returning to duties or on the way out to a welcome few days' leave, whenever possible they were found a seat and frequently cosseted beyond the flight itself, sharing detachment transport or even found the luxury of a bath or room. For those who had done their stint it was an escape to a kinder world.

As one American nutrition co-ordinator said: "It is easier to hop on one of these than wait for a civilian flight. I was stranded in Makalle for two days. Then the RAF brought me back."

The crews would sometimes find themselves confronted by Sisters of Charity leading one or two bewildered children, with or without the small carrier bag that contained their pitiful belongings. Orphaned by the famine, the children had been accepted by one of the orphanages in or near Addis Ababa. They were handed over, frightened and wide-eyed with wonder, to the care of the loadmasters, many of them family men, who knew exactly how to bring smiles to tearful faces. The ration boxes were raided for biscuits, sweets, orange juice and milk powder (which the children liked to eat!) and the waifs were kept happy by crew and airmovers alike until they were handed over to waiting nuns at Bole Airport.

Skills and training in aeromedical evacuation would be called on when answering a plea from one of the desert clinics to transport a seriously sick patient to a city hospital. It could be a relief worker suddenly taken ill, or a mother or child or an elderly Ethiopian, ravaged and debilitated by starvation, whose only hope was treatment in a modern hospital bed. The Hercules, which had been humping grain all day, became a flying ambulance on the homeward journey, with the crew bunk on the flight deck turned over to the casualty, or stretchers laid on the floor or fastened to the line of bucket seats.

There were many notable passengers taken on fact finding flights including Government ministers, UN, embassy and relief agency officials. The most famous of all was Mother Theresa of Calcutta who was flown by Flight Lieutenants Martin Oxborrow and Andy Swift to Makalle. She expected to be flown back to Addis in an aircraft from another source, but late in the afternoon while on a grain delivery the crew received a transmitted message from an Asmara based Red Cross flight that she was stranded. So they diverted in flight to Makalle and brought her back to Bole Airport. They will always remember her charm, caring nature and ready wit. Needless to say she inveigled them into spare-time involvement – assistance in preparation of some plans for a new mission in Addis Ababa. Her tireless, diminutive sisters in their white robes with blue-bordered headdress and open sandals could be found everywhere, in the thick of the battle against famine.

Martin also carried a Live Aid film crew on an Addis Ababa-Assab-Alamata supply shuttle, and his crew were filmed helping the locals off-load 1,400 tins of high nutrition biscuits. Other flights were accompanied by BBC, ITN, Red Cross, Swiss TV and Band Aid film teams, and many world accredited journalists.

Far more terrifying and traumatic to simple upcountry people were the resettlement flights undertaken by the Russians and other East Bloc air forces from the northern provinces and Eritrea to southern Ethiopia. Resettlement

Crew and passengers of an RAF Hercules, watched by their 'minder' (leaning against the vehicle) at Assab as they gather to board the aircraft for a flight to Makalle.
Photo author

in itself is not an evil policy, in fact a number of nations, Indonesia as an example, have successfully uprooted people from homelands which have suffered desertification to a more fertile part of the country. However, most of the Western nations totally condemned the Ethiopian Relief and Rehabilitation Commission's deportation of 250,000 people, 86,000 of them from Tigre alone, not for the scheme in itself but for the way in which it was executed and its geo-political reasons – to depopulate regions where secession was strongly supported. Some United Nations observers endeavoured to persuade the Western nations that, non-politically, it was as good a solution as any, and UN co-ordinator Kurt Jansson urged the West to support it. Some made a new life for themselves in a greener, pleasanter world within a more predictable rainbelt, and the opposition was attacked by the RRC, which worked hard and struggled to make it a success, as "politicising humanitarian efforts".

But in northern areas of heavy insubordination people were airlifted away, not so much because of the shortage of food but because they were believed to be succouring rebel troops. In one region where the rest of the world was endeavouring to pour grain and other foodstuffs it was alleged that the few mean crops which had reached maturity had actually been destroyed by Government troops as an act of war. It was also claimed that there were suitable areas much nearer the homelands, that the long, traumatic journeys were unnecessary.

When the resettlement programme was initiated the Ethiopian Government started moving people overland in caravans of battered buses and lorries along inhospitable tracks and roads. The journey was uncomfortable, slow and tortuous, there were no contingency plans for food and shelter, and the caravans were not nearly fast enough for their purpose. The major part of the airborne deportation programme was undertaken by the Russians and it soon became apparent that many of the mysterious absences of the Bole-based Aeroflot An-12 Cubs were on resettlement flights. From brooding in lines opposite the British Military Detachment headquarters, there was a sudden increase in activity, and the morning shift would arrive to find that, whereas the night before there had been a fleet of Cubs, now there was an empty pan.

There were disturbing accounts as to how the airlift was accomplished – of terrified and pathetic people being lined up and coerced at gunpoint on to the transport aircraft, with families frequently split (a later survey estimating that fifteen per cent had been separated from close relatives). There were no seats on the aircraft and the passengers were packed into the unpressurised hold

Big brother keeps watch. A Soviet operated MI-8 Hip calls on its Polish counterpart in a remote upland area in Wollo. Photo author

Entente Cordiale. German, British and Swedish crews get together on the pan at Addis Ababa. Photo Stu Bailey

like sardines in a tin and treated less kindly than living cattle. It was said that one or two incredibly callous Soviet crews climbed above 20,000 feet in the knowledge that the malnourished passengers, weakened by disease and dysentery, would be beyond redemption. It was not then within Soviet ideology to question a hard and distasteful task, but in fairness, most Russian crews did not subject their unwilling passengers to such extremes. Some people had never even seen an aeroplane before, much less been forcibly flown in one. The flights were traumatic enough without the added agonies of hypoxia.

What was even more disturbing was a report that some mercy flights were being used as a means to attract and trick people with a promise of free food towards the feeding camps and drop zones, where they were rounded up and forced into Russian-operated Hips. Health workers spoke of screams in the night, of abject people, terrified of the scything rotors, crawling at gunpoint towards the aircraft on their knees.

The authorities took great precautions to hide what was being done. At first few members of the detachment saw the full horrors of the resettlement flights. Police guards or a couple of engineers toiling overnight to produce an airworthy Hercules for the morning grain run would hear the Antonovs taxiing in and see the hundreds of world-weary passengers being shepherded or carried down the ramp in the dim lights of the aircraft hold – then hear the airport fire engines moving in with all speed to hose down the interior – mute testament to the suffering of these people in flight. As resettlement intensified the flights extended into the daylight hours and it became a visual, upsetting reminder to all as to why the detachment was there. The British crews did not envy the Soviet airmen their job.

Kurt Jansson was the first to point out to Colonel Mengistu that the scheme had been poorly planned and haphazardly carried out. There were claims by Western relief agencies as the numbers deported passed 1,500,000 that more Ethiopians died as a result of the resettlement policy than died of famine. However, the RRC insisted that a total of 89,664 families had been successfully moved by air to different parts of the country.

At the height of the rehabilitation scheme an East German and a Libyan An-26 arrived at Bole, parking near the main terminal. However, the Libyan aircraft sat on the pan for a week or ten days, moved a token number of people and on one occasion its crew borrowed a RAF forklift to load some food. This aircraft did not stay long.

The Soviets evacuated casualties of war from the beleaguered northern provinces. Most had been airlifted out of the battle zones by Ethiopian Air Force Hips. Actively engaged in combating extensive guerilla activity by Eritrean forces and Tigrean rebels, the Ethiopian Air Force operated a mish-mash of aircraft types most, but by no means all, Soviet-built aircraft and flown by Cuban and Russian crews and advisers. Hopelessly in debt to its ally, Ethiopia relied on Russian back-up to fly the wounded to Asmara or Addis Ababa. The city hospitals were full of the wounded, though local people were never told from where they had come. As hostilities increased in the north the sight of stretchers and walking wounded being disgorged from helicopters and An-12s became a common sight to relief flyers.

Another resettlement programme which will go down in the annals of aviation and Ethiopia was the flight of the Falashas.

In neighbouring Sudan problems of drought, famine and political unrest were accelerating, not least because many thousands of Ethiopian refugees were fleeing from the persecution of their own regime over a wild, inhospitable frontier which was impossible to patrol. Most of them hoped for nothing more than some food and freedom from harrassment. But for the Falashas, a tribe with Jewish beliefs in a country steeped in ancient religious creeds, it was a different story. Simple highland desert people, mostly from Tigre and Gondar, they ex-

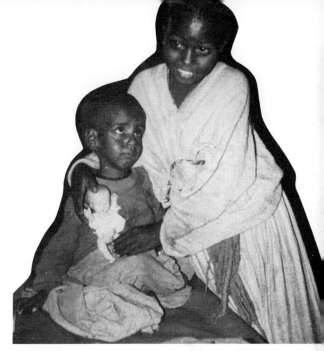

A present from England. One of the gifts that Stu Bailey brought for the children of Makalle.
Photo Stu Bailey

pected that Old Testament prophecies would come to pass and that there would be an exodus to a promised land. And for them, this is what happened. Incredibly, organised by the Israeli secret service Mossad, 28,000 Falashas made a long and secret trek into Sudan, many of them believing that over the border was Jerusalem. But from here, with a blind-eye condonation from the Sudanese who did not want the refugees, they were airlifted to Israel in what became known as 'Operation Moses'.

The flights, organised by the Belgian charter firm, Trans European Airlines, were in Boeing 707s which had been used in regular flights from Sudan to Mecca, carrying pilgrims. They started on November 21st 1984 in great secrecy and during six weeks over 7,000 Falashas were airlifted from Khartoum to Ben Gurion Airport, Tel Aviv, before a furious Ethiopian Government twigged what was going on.

After thirty-five flights were completed (routed via Brussels or Rome for diplomatic reasons and quietly backed up by an Israeli Air Force Hercules) the secret airlift was abruptly halted on January 5th when someone leaked the story to the Jewish Press – to the great consternation of the Ethiopian Jews already in Israel, and causing rows within the Israeli Government. The mercy

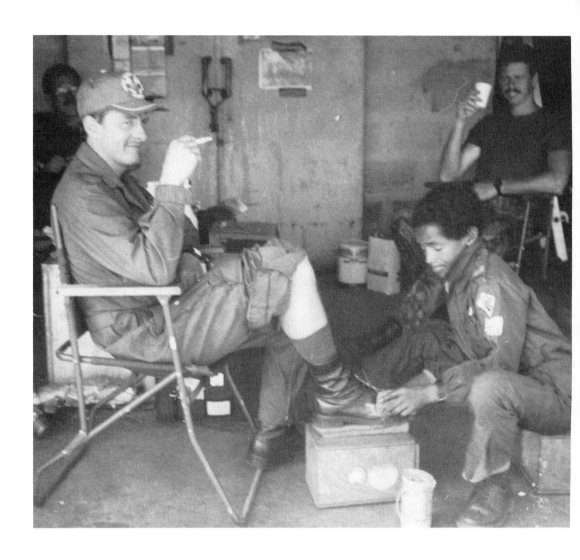

flights were coming to a peak and it was expected that the 12,000 left behind who had survived the trek and wanted to join their people in Israel would be moved during the following week. There were more secret talks between various nations and a number of airlines willing to continue the airlift. It was quietly collated and completed by the Jewish agency, Zvi Eyal within the next few weeks.

*   *   *

The first six months of Operation Bushel were drawing to a close – and there was no let-up. Flying hours had exceeded 1,500 and the two Hercules had ferried over 31 million pounds of grain and supplies. It seemed incredible to airmen on all the mercy flights, working

Waiting for 'Albert'. Engineer Sgt Peter Begley gets a shoeshine in the leisure tent from Girma, the 'detachment mascot'. Photo author

against the clock to fill their enormous aircraft to the limits with food, and humping it on the numerous shuttles, seven days a week, that there were still so many hungry people. But now that more and more were able to visit the feeding centres this was plain to see, and even more apparent on the drop zones where some villages had previously been so inaccessible that, apart from the valiant but intermittent mission light aircraft and helicopters bringing in what they could, they had just been forgotten by their own Government and the outside world.

Every visitor to the feeding centres arrived with gifts, as much as he or she could carry, small medical supplies, notebooks, pencils or toys for the children. 'Stu' Bailey, a Master Airloadmaster with LXX Squadron visited Makalle on his rest day. A veteran of Middle and Far East action, Northern Ireland and the Falklands, he admitted that no operation had made the same impact on him as the Ethiopian mercy flights.

"I got a bit of a shaker. At Makalle eighteen nuns from different religious orders were running a camp with about 40,000 people inside and another 40,000 waiting to come in. In a hospital tent I saw people suffering from typhoid, typhus, cholera, spinal TB, cancer, polio and scabies as well as malnutrition and dehydration. There were terrible sights. Flies laid eggs inside peoples' eyelids, pus formed and the eyes were eaten away."

He had arrived with 4,000 pens and 200 notebooks for the nuns' little schools, given by people and schools in his home town, 300 tennis balls (a sports firm had donated 6,000, suitable for the climate, when returning crews reported that the children had nothing to play with) and some dolls. The refugees crowded round and he was introduced by one of the nursing sisters as "the man from the sky who brought grain." The Ethiopian peasants have their own way of saying 'thank you' – a high ululation of the throat, like a Red Indian war-whoop.

"It sounded as if all 40,000 were making this whooping sound – quite incredible and very moving", said Stu, adding: "I was naive, expecting to hand it all out myself. But the nuns knew best who could benefit. They were so marvellous – and they called us the angels of mercy!"

He was particularly impressed with the efforts to encourage people in simple hygiene.

"Countrymen in Ethiopia don't normally labour. They will plough, but the women labour. The nun in charge, Sister Sheila, had so much incredible drive she convinced the men to dig latrines down to bedrock with basic instruments. When she smiled and said they were the best men ever, they all clapped. She organised best tent competitions, best clean areas, best water channel and planting areas."

Like everyone else he had seen the poignant television news films and asked himself: "Is the grain and money getting through to the people who need it?"

He discovered that it was, and that once people in the camp were healthier they did not have to be asked to help.

"It kept us going all through those hard days of airdropping and land delivery. You knew that every pound of grain you landed was another person's life for a day."

At Lyneham everyone who had skills to contribute had volunteered. By now, for some members of the British detachment, it was second time around. They were heartened to see the results, the milled grain being cooked, chirpier children, and people using and wearing the blankets and clothing from the Hercules and aircraft chartered by the public which they had unloaded in the very early days of Operation Bushel.

Bob Jones returned on a second stint and visited the irrigation project at Bulbulo which he and his colleagues had initiated together with Save the Children. Ground engineers, on their days off, rebuilt the kitchens of one of Mother Theresa's orphanages and repaired the incubators at the Black Lion Hospital.

Major Batty, who managed the 47 AD Squadron members' fund for Save the Children, (which had come to his rescue when he needed an underwriter for a quick delivery of sacks), approached the suppliers of airdropping equipment. He was rewarded with a donation of £10,300 from Bridport Aviation, who provided sacks and cord, and generous contributions from other suppliers. The squadron 'adopted' the Bethesda Orphanage at Debre Zeit, thirty miles south of Addis. An arc welder was purchased to rewire the faulty electrical system at the orphanage and several hundredweights of food were delivered. With the help of other agencies a four-wheel-drive truck was delivered overland.

One lucky beneficiary was Girma, an eleven-year-old Ethiopian boy who, among numerous hangers-on at the airport, had made himself indispensable, making tea and doing odd jobs, and becoming a sort of detachment mascot. On hearing that his family were too poor to send him to school, one of the pilots sponsored his education.

CHAPTER THIRTEEN

Tales from the Drop Zones

IN April, as more drop zones were brought into use, the air-drop Hercules was flying three sorties a day and despatching a total of one million pounds of grain every ten days. The landing aeroplane was delivering the same amount every week, the two RAF aircraft flying an average of ten hours a day altogether. But now food was getting to remote areas hitherto unreached, and up to 10,000 people could frequently be seen waiting patiently beside each DZ for their food to arrive. The small safety team and off-duty personnel who spent the day on the DZ would find themselves amongst the people in their own environment – most of them undernourished, their dried-out bodies ill-clad in ratty clothes or blankets, their eyes large with hunger. The steady exodus from the villages was halting, easing the pressures on the centres. The RRC's reluctance had turned to enthusiasm, for shrewdly they realised also that the 'ring of starvation' which had come as close as ten miles from the capital city, traditionally the place where hungry peasants headed, was now receding.

In spite of efforts by local officials to control the hordes, streams of people would converge towards the DZs, greedy to get the first supplies. Many had travelled long distances. The hope in their faces as they watched the aviators work formed an unforgettable picture of misery. But the most harrowing sight of all was at the end of the day – from the comfort of Hercules and Transall flightdecks or helicopter hold as the flyers turned for home – the gleaners descending in their hundreds on to the DZ, squatting on their haunches and brushing up the precious spilt corn with small twigs and tufts of brushwood, throwing it in the air to get rid of the dust.

In the midst of all this, air crews and safety crews alike had to concentrate on procedures and standards expected of everyone during their thirty-odd sorties while on detachment. An air despatch examining team from No. 1 Group Upavon was sent out to invigilate in air-to-ground operations, and there was frequently an instructor with both dropping and ground crews. The constant rigorous training paid off. German and British crews flew in each others' aircraft, compared notes and learnt from each other. There were many valuable lessons, for both present and future operations.

The safety officer on the DZ was responsible for all air and ground space and no dropping was permitted until cleared by him. Controlling the crowds, by sheer weight of numbers, was not easy. Even Rabel, which had been well ordered at first, became difficult. It was as if, now that they were sure that the food would not get into rebel hands, the RRC had become somewhat complacent. Inevitably there were accidents, occasionally fatal or serious, when someone would evade control, anxious for his own small piece of loot. It was even known for people to crouch down on the DZ, camouflaged in their brown blankets against the ochre groundscape, waiting to 'catch' their own bag of corn. One man died when hit by a fifty-six pound bag of corn travelling at 160 miles per hour. On another sortie a captain had to initiate an overshoot when he saw something brown, crouched and moving, directly below. Others would get too near the dropping area and be hit by a bouncing sack, or a piece of broken pallet would ricochet into the crowd. People tended to start running towards the DZ before things had come to a standstill. Everything had a value and was eagerly utilised. Small pieces of pallet became precious fuel for cooking fires, a larger piece would be seized to reinforce the wall of a tokul. Broken corners of sacks became sunhats or clothing or were used to block out the cold in someone's living area.

The local authorities were not slow in taking advantage of the large gatherings of people to hold political meetings, generally conducted during the interval between the arrival of each air dropping aircraft. These consisted of a loud harangue by megaphone and ended with communal shouts in support of the Government, an incongruous performance to flyers and relief workers alike, who took care not to get involved.

The Polish and Helimission crews provided transport for site surveys, their white helicopters a visible landmark for inbound transports. Some DZs were selected beside a small airstrip, where the ground was known to be level and light aircraft were handy for onward transportation.

The sign language, basic aviation English and smiles which passed for communication between the safety teams and the Polish crews were enhanced when Sergeant Bob Szafran, a Polish-speaking member of the

Air Despatch Squadron, joined the detachment and became a splendid link man between the two. Unfortunately he was taken ill and had to be flown home. Worried that lack of a translator might bring about a pull-out, though far from recovered, he insisted on flying back to Ethiopia to carry on the good work (he was awarded a BEM in the 1986 New Year Honours List). Another member of the safety crew, Staff Sergeant Paul Shenton, who had joined the team from the Army School of Transport in Aldershot to make video records, will always be remembered by one thirteen-year-old Ethiopian mother. While he was on duty on a DZ the girl went into labour and was obviously having difficulties. He delivered her baby and, aware that the placenta had not been freed and unhappy about her condition, insisted on a casevac for her in the helicopter to an Addis hospital.

On all the drop zones there were always hordes of children and tolerance was expected of safety teams and visitors who commonly found themselves surrounded by youngsters hopeful of a sweet or biscuit and eager to practise their English. This was often surprisingly good, and British servicemen discovered the answers to many day-to-day queries, learning about Ethiopia from the mouths of the children. One reference, to the 'yellow house', baffled them for some time, especially when the children said they were forbidden to enter. But it turned out to be nothing more sinister than the local 'pub' where the country beer 'tej' (which is yellow) was brewed from the gayshu leaf and imbibed.

Air-dropping at Shil Afaf, where the bulk of food was to arrive by RAF Hercules.
Photo Jim Gilchrist

Shil Afaf – taking grain from drop to feeding centre past Polish helicopter. Photo author

Climbing away at Derek Amba. Photo author

The first of new drop zones to be utilised was at Shil Afaf, eighty miles north-west of Addis Ababa, near the Wollo border. The survey team, having mapped and recced the zone, came back with a recommendation that it was not suitable for air despatch as the ground was so hard and stony. But the British and German detachment commanders were persuaded to try it by RRC officials because it was an area of great deprivation.

Each new DZ had its own characteristics. At Shil Afaf, wild and beautiful, the challenges caused by similar terrain to that at Rabel were accentuated by mid-day turbulence, as Brian Nicolle discovered on one of the initial air drops. The straight run-in on 320° magnetic was over a ravine and a small group of tokuls and trees about one and a half miles from the DZ. Over the tiny hamlet convection currents hit the aircraft so violently that the load was thrown off its conveyor rails. He held off while the load was relocated, flying very gently over the valley. An angled approach, lining up with the DZ at the very last moment, was the only way to avoid a repeat performance. It was so small that it was a navigator's nightmare. Drop too soon and the load went into a ridge, drop too late and it could disappear down a ravine.

Under the realigned glide path was a small medical camp, run in rotation by various international health teams. When air-dropping started, a Canadian team was in residence. The nurses had fixed themselves a shower area, screened off by plastic but open at the top, fondly known as 'Sun World'. On hearing the Hercules approach they would dive into 'Sun World', strip off their clothes and wave to the crews.

"Our lifestyle was bizarre and circumstances were such that they tended to engender quirks of behaviour", commented Dr Jim Gilchrist, the medical director.

It was said that one Hercules approach was so low that it took the top off one of the trees! Flowers and chocolates arrived on a small parachute.

Their strip show was emulated one day by air despatchers who, hearing that there were some so-called 'VIPs' among the helicopter party promised something spectacular at the end of the drop. The 'show' was an irreverent line of bare bottoms, hanging over the ramp as the Hercules climbed away!

At Shil Afaf there had been virtually no food at all, except that brought in by light aircraft or helicopter. The bulk of it was now to arrive by Hercules.

"Without it, no way would many people have been fed. There were so many very malnourished people, children and adults, in the small intensified feeding centre", said Jim Gilchrist.

One day, he and an American nurse made the half-hour walk to the DZ. The feeding centre had not been open for two days.

"The mass of humanity was astonishing – about 5,000 people on the slope, the whole length of the DZ, many from over the Wollo border. Chaos reigned. We saw the difficulties of controlling the zone – it was a reminder of the tenuous state of the food supply and how people react to a sudden influx of food. Shil Afaf people did not get their full share that day", he said.

The landing party from the Polish helicopter were surprised to see two bedraggled westerners and gave them what remained of their lunches, fruit and biscuits.

"We were very grateful as we had very little to eat and there had been no helicopter support for two days", Jim recalled.

The next DZ to be used was at Seyo, ninety-four miles from Addis in Western Shewa, halfway down the Blue Nile valley. Its 900 yards usable length was surrounded by tall trees from forty to sixty feet high on the 020° run-in, chosen to give an approach over flat terrain rather than rising ground.

Wing Commander Steve Wrigley, 47 Squadron commander and a 'Khana Cascade' veteran succeeded Wing Commander Nicolle as detachment commander, to be followed by Wing Commander Roger Green, who commanded the Operations Wing at Lyneham. Both found, by now, that administration and routine were running smoothly, with much of the early ideological confrontations ironed out. The sheer efficiency of the operation,

while he expected it, greatly impressed Roger Green, whose primary role, so far, had been to monitor homecoming aircraft. He spent as much time as he could spare flying with RAF and Polish crews to see for himself conditions and results.

Visiting some of the feeding camps, he too marvelled at the discipline and culture of Ethiopians in adversity.

"I saw at Makalle the kids who were to be fed on one side of a low wall, and the adults on the other. They did not cross. Each family had their 'house' marked out in the bare earth with a ring of stones", he recalled.

Flying with the Polish Relief Squadron produced some lighter moments. One day he accompanied an executive Wing Commander from Lyneham who had come to Addis to monitor administration, when the officer was invited by sign language to fly the helicopter. He was duly installed in the captain's seat and left, heading along a valley towards an enormous cliff. With great difficulty he got through to the crew that he was not a pilot and didn't know what to do next!

Watching the sacks and pallets fly.
Air Despatchers on the RAF Hercules ramp.
Photo Geoff Whyham RAF

The Poles were extremely hospitable and it was difficult to refuse invitations to take 'tea' with them at the end of the day. Members of the British detachment soon became aware that, if their transport was not there, this usually degenerated into a vodka session in the Polish Colonel's tent.

Roger Green vividly remembers his own experience:

"We were invited to the Colonel's tent through his interpreter, to take tea. We were welcomed by two Polish Colonels, with bread, meat and glasses, and offered coffee or tea. Then a toast was proposed by the Colonel in command and we were asked whether we would like vodka or pure grain spirit. Realising we were representing Queen and Country, we elected vodka. The amounts were generous, a large bottle filling five glasses.

"Then the second Colonel proposed a toast, after which it was my turn, and that of my deputy. Then the Colonel produced his own special brew and invited us to try it – a mixture of half vodka, a quarter pure spirit and a quarter honey. We held our own, all in the space of an hour and a half, but were grateful to be driven home by the interpreter."

It was quietly arranged that, for the future, the transport minibus would be there and waiting!

Not the chorus line from "It 'Aint 'Arf 'Ot, Mum" but a team of cheerful air despatchers demonstrating their skills! (from left), Drivers Colin Donkin, Andrew Johnstone, Craig Jones and their leader Cpl Kevin Jones. Photo author

In the early days of air-dropping it became the custom for the landing party's lunch and hot water for drinks to be dropped in a harness pack by small parachute. Then the Poles decided to takeover the midday catering, producing daily a delectable picnic of varied meats and light and floury Russian bread, baked in their field kitchens (it was grudgingly admitted that this was something that the Soviets could do better than the British!).

*   *   *

Trials of new equipment were held on the DZs. For the first time grain was packed in polypropylene sacks made by Courtaulds, who had taken part in a successful trial drop in England. At Meranya, one of the earliest drop zones to be used, a test drop of sixteen pallets was undertaken with Courtauld's sacks, with a ninety-eight per cent success rate. Only ten burst out of a total of 368 sacks,

Air drop sacks used to block out the cold in a nurse's bedroom at the Shil Afaf medical camp.
Photo Jim Gilchrist

and fifty-five per cent were recovered for use. This was a culmination for the manufacturer of a production programme which started in 1968 when a heavy plastic material was produced on the cotton looms at Talbot Mills, Chorley, Lancashire to replace jute and made into bags to carry one-ton loads of toxic necessities such as chemicals, fertilisers or cement for heavy industry. The tough, durable material was ideal for heavy dropping and from then on until near the end of the operation it was used exclusively for outer protection, the company supplying 140,000 sacks for air dropping. They were also supplied to the Luftwaffe, and to the Belgian Air Force on request from the Red Cross. At Gundo Meskel there was a successful experiment with the heatshrink plastic covers which were used from then on during the remainder of the airlift.

All the drop zones had so far been in northern Shewa. That the need was just as great in southern Wollo was evident from the streams of people who arrived daily on the DZs from over the province border. The UN were anxious for air dropping to be extended into the Central Ethiopian Highlands, but this had been vetoed by the Ethiopian Government because of enemy activity and the fear that food would be diverted into rebel hands. The area was also limited to the range of the Polish helicopters. However on April 18th a four-day survey was started by a multi-national party in the RRC Cessna Centurion

over areas where there had been known fighting just a month before. There was no evidence of any security problems.

Three areas in southern Wollo were found to be suitable for air-dropping and well within helicopter range – at Derek Amba, Ajibar and Lemi. The local militia agreed to protect the Polish helicopter if the need should arise and also to help control the crowds.

Derek Amba was the first DZ to be selected in Wollo. This was difficult to find because they had been given the wrong co-ordinates; the first Polish crew became lost and the Hercules arrived before them and directed them in by radio. Ready for any contingency because of recent history, crews had been issued with flak jackets and told to be on special alert. The sight of the local militia, armed to the teeth with a motley array of weapons from the turn of the century to modern Kalashnikovs, though there for their protection, was daunting enough! However, proceedings were well ordered – to everyone's amazement quite highly organised by an eighteen-year-old Ethiopian girl employed by the RRC. Turn any corner, and Ethiopia was full of surprises.

A tremendous amount of grain was to be dropped at

Lemi, a catchment area for about 100,000 people. The DZ was 100 nautical miles due north of Addis Ababa, nearly 8,000 feet high with a usable length of 1,000 yards and a preferred run-in on 212°(m), the run-out between two villages and over a dirt road in a north-south direction. There was an appalling drop just before the threshold into a seemingly bottomless canyon. Somewhere in the depths below there was a river bed.

Ajibar is about fifty miles west from the inland city of Dessie, on the slopes of almost impenetrable mountain country. Two drop zones were selected and named respectively Ajibar East and Ajibar West. Ajibar East, 9,000 feet above sea level, was situated about halfway to Dessie. It had a steep approach, 300 feet high ridges on either side and a 6,000 feet gorge at the end of the run. It was always surrounded by people and had a small village of

Precious grains. An Ethiopian girl epitomises the tragedy of her country as she gleans for her family at Gundo Meskel.
Photo Geoff Whyham RAF

Controlling the DZ. Staff Sgt Dave Collie of 47 Air Despatch Squadron clears the Hercules to drop.
Photo Geoff Whyham RAF

A full load of eight clusters in the RAF Hercules.
Photo Dany Gignoux ICRC

trees and huts in the undershoot area. Dropping had to be delayed until late over the DZ to avoid accidental damage resulting from an early release. Most of the grain dropped here was for storage. Ajibar West, where there was a large World Vision feeding centre, was used as the main point for food distribution to 150,000 people living in the mountains and gorges. Even the staff had been reduced to surviving on fried potatoes, until Hercules and Transalls arrived. Twenty-one miles from Lemi, at 9,510 feet this was the highest DZ to be utilised during Operation Bushel. It lay on a ridge to the east of a number of tree-lined highland villages and its usable length of 800 yards was on a recommended run-in, run-out, track of 303°(m). The DZ itself was grassed and firm but it was littered with boulders. It had a ten degrees upslope with trees forty feet high at the far end. Pilots were warned.

The Wollo DZs seemed even more hairy than those in Shewa. Each one appeared to be either broached or escape-routed over a bottomless pit, each threshold and climb-out surrounded by trees, surprisingly high in such barren terrain. Local people did their best to clear the flightpath, but there were the inevitable treestrikes, birdstrikes, the occasional collapse of a grass-roofed tokul in the slipstream. Mechanical problems were, happily, few though one Hercules developed a major prop leak from No 2 engine while over Ajibar. When the

crew heard that there was no chance of a replacement propeller at Addis until the arrival of the resupply aircraft this Hercules was flown north with its defect to Asmara to borrow a prop from Transamerica Airlines.

But in spite of all, the flying retained its magic – from walking out to the aircraft as the light came up from nowhere to walking away exhausted and exhilarated as it faded as quickly as it had come. No-where else in the world had there been such an opportunity to practise skilled 'on the-deck' cross-country and precision flying, over a dun-coloured land to a mountain dream world of spectacular awe. The ridges raced by, one minute below, the next minute above, a tilting panorama as the aircraft turned. The summits in the path of the aircraft fell away, so close underneath as if being caressed by the fuselage underbody, as if one could lean out and touch the bare rock; then a black nothingness as the earth plunged to some mysterious depths of its own below. The magnificent aeroplanes put their shoulders to the load, each a burdened Pegasus. It was an experience which no-one on the Hercules squadrons would have missed.

But the greatest challenge of all was still to come.

CHAPTER FOURTEEN

Rain

THE 'small rains' began to appear as early as the last days of March. After three years of uninterrupted drought and nine of inadequate rainfall, they were a message of 'tesfa' for the Ethiopian people and their arid and thirsty land. For the flyers they were a foreboding of things to come.

At first the change was intermittent but even then it could be sudden and violent as Flight Lieutenant Peter Butler and a 47 Squadron crew discovered one day in late March. They set out in the early afternoon with a load of supplies for Gondar in all too familiar blue skies and puffs of strato-cumulus. After unloading the aircraft at Gondar an engine refused to start with a sheared starter motor. While they squatted on the strip and the engineers struggled, the visibility deteriorated alarmingly and they found themselves surrounded by spectacular thunderstorms. They were very relieved at the sight of the airdrop Hercules, coming to their rescue captained by Squadron Leader Andy Clarke with a LXX Squadron crew,

who gave them a 'buddy-buddy' start. Both aircraft climbed through a 25,000 feet density of 'active' cunim cloud to overfly what was fast developing into a tempest. It was a telling example of how normal mechanical problems can be compounded by the weather.

However, despite deteriorating flying conditions during April and May momentum was maintained. There was a feeling of a race against time, not only to feed hungry mouths, but because grain was sitting in the open – and no-one knew quite how much flying was going to be affected in the future. Already there could be dust at one end of a flight and rain-sodden runways at the other. As the last long blow of the dry north-east tradewinds was superseded by air currents from the moist south-east

The main rains arrive with a vengeance.
Grounded by weather XV209 squats forlornly by
a puddle on the parking bay at Addis Ababa.
Photo Geoff Whyham RAF

there was added motivation in that increasingly some cargoes of food grain were being replaced by seed, wheat and barley at first, then maize, teff (millet) and sorghum, much of it supplied by the USA, EEC and Canada, to replace that which had been eaten, and to enable people to return to their farms. Flights were also undertaken at the request of the Ethiopian Government to neighbouring African countries which were supplying seed corn. During April two Hercules loads of pickaxes were delivered to Metemma and similar agricultural aids flown to other strips to break the hard-baked land, some of it left fallow for several years by farmers too weak to work. Oxen, behind whose patient yoke the rural economy had traditionally sown its crops, were greatly missed. Now, in most areas tillage was a struggling partnership between man and the tiny long-suffering Ethiopian ass, amazingly resilient for its size to drought and the labours imposed on it.

In many parts of the country the food situation was still

Bales of blankets for cold, wet people, wait to be loaded at Addis Ababa while running repairs are undertaken to a leading edge after a birdstrike. Photo Geoff Whyham RAF

The heatshrink plastic more than proved its worth in the wet season. Air Despatcher Lance Corporal Pete Marsden uses a heat gun to fasten and waterproof the seams. Photo Geoff Whyham RAF

critical. UN co-ordinator Kurt Jansson estimated that, with the problems of terrain, civil war and now rain, only about thirty-six per cent of the monthly requirement of food was being distributed, and most of that in the feeding camps, which held but a minority of the starving population. In May he suggested that both RAF Hercules concentrate on air dropping, but by the middle of the month the store-houses in Addis Ababa were beginning to run dry, some of the shortage caused by water damage to road and rail links from the ports. As June approached there was evidence that the long overdue main rains were imminent. There was that sweet and special smell in the air of parched earth suddenly refreshed by a south-west monsoon. A dun-coloured world turned brown. The familiar twelve hour day of blue skies and burning sun was drastically curtailed as lowering cloud began to add to the 'normal' hazards encountered. Misty early mornings and heavy rain in the afternoon became the pattern.

Wing Commander Wrigley was the first detachment commander to have to cope with Ethiopian weather extremes. Lowering cloud, poor visibility and thunderstorms began seriously to affect flying, reducing the freedom to operate in VFR conditions. Flying techniques and dropping skills were continually reassessed. He decreed that free drop would continue as long as there was grain to deliver and as long as the DZs could be reached under or through the cloud cover. Other IMC flights at mountain DZ altitudes were not considered prudent in the dearth of accurate navaids. It was not uncommon to divert up to twenty-five miles off track around thunderstorms to reach a DZ, the Herc's white landing light looming out of the murk over canyon or ridge the first warning that it had arrived. Sometimes alternative locations were searched out, in exhausting conditions demanding both skill and stamina from crews and despatchers. But a number of air drops had to be cancelled.

Colonel Escheti, the stalwart RRC co-ordinator, left for Canada to take delivery of and pilot home a Twin Otter which had been presented to the RRC by the relief agency World Vision. His duties were taken over by Colonel Tsegaye, already controlling relief helicopter operations at Addis and well aware of the problems facing his bureaucratic government, trying to run the country and fight the war with acute shortage of cash.

Two more DZs were brought into use in addition to the ten already established. These were at Chisa and Begide, both east of the central northern air-dropping area. Begide, at an altitude of 8,500 feet had an ample wide plateau, 2,000 yards long. With a recommended run-in on 110°(m), it had a dirt access road at the end of the DZ, speeding up clearance in doubtful weather. Chisa, nearly 9,000 feet up, was in spectacular mountain terrain though it also had an unpaved road to the north. The flight to Chisa was across the Great Rift Valley canyons to head up Three Falls Valley over rims of vertical canyon walls, some of the most wild and beautiful scenery that the crews were to fly over. There was a 250 feet summit to clear just forty-five seconds from the target and a high degree of accuracy necessary, for the DZ itself was only 80 yards wide with a 1,500 yards length of parched earth.

The seasonal problems were even worse for air landing crews. The sudden violent downpours could waterlog strips in minutes, turning soil into mud. At Makalle and Assab there was no drainage and pilots could find themselves landing in large pools of water. Airfields could close down suddenly because of the state of the runway. Maps and previous operational data could be invalidated by the rain. Six or seven major birdstrikes were experienced during the rainy season. But flying operations were even more vital with road and rail links washed away. On the quaysides the grain was beginning to rot. There were never enough tarpaulins.

Around Addis Ababa the main rains began to arrive with a vengeance. Alamata, the only major airstrip to serve two large feeding centres, Alamata and Korem, became waterlogged and unusable. In spite of a previous day's recce which showed no signs of deterioration Martin Oxborrow and his crew experienced soft strip problems. After unloading, their Hercules was reluctant to accelerate to TAC VR (rotate speed) because of drag imposed by the surface. When the Herc was unwillingly airborne, a vibration was felt in the airframe which was subsequently found to be caused by a damaged main landing gear door, the result of contact with the deep and mushy ground. The strip had to be declared unusable until it dried out. However, flying continued into Assab, Axum and the rocky based Makalle and Gondar which were marginally less affected by wet weather, though flooding at Assab contaminated fuel, to the dismay of all the heavy relief operators.

For movers and despatchers, rain caused logistical problems. When it came it was generally heavy. The sacks had to be speedily covered, but inevitably some got wet. A wet sack of grain can weigh up to fifty per cent more than a dry one, leading to a dramatic revision in payload calculations. The heatshrink plastic more than proved its worth in protecting the assembled clusters. Courtauld's polypropylene sacks were also waterproof, though wet could seep in at the stitching. A number of tents were hastily rustled up by the RRC and erected beside detachment headquarters to provide somewhat inadequate shelter.

The Luftwaffe crews were also experiencing weather related vicissitudes and some of their own, because of the company they kept at Dire Dawa. Returning from air dropping on May 12th late in the afternoon they found a cyclone centred over the airfield. Lacking enough fuel to divert, they prepared to brave it, but having been cleared to land ten miles out by Air Traffic Control, they were dismayed to hear ATC clear a Soviet An-12 'twelve miles out' and coming from the opposite direction. Having endured the Russians' disinclination to use aviation English but long suspecting that their radio operators could understand, they were not completely surprised to be answered when they bypassed Dire Dawa ATC and called the Russian aircraft direct. With no possibility of either of them holding in a storm-tossed circuit and the risk of a mid-air collision at stake they decided between themselves that, as the Transall was faster and had reverse thrust, it would land first while the Soviet pilot would apply full flap and reduce speed. The Transall crew duly landed, turning off the runway with all haste, only to see the An-12 appearing out of the murk and landing from the opposite direction just 50 yards away. As it roared past the crews exchanged thumbs up signals!

It was ironic that, for the Ethiopian people, the life-giving rains brought the inevitable consequences of extremes of climate and a misery if anything more physical than that caused by drought. There was massive erosion with roads and topsoil and newly sown seeds washed away or rotted because of too much water. The formerly dried-up gullies and watercourses, difficult enough to traverse in the dry season, became impassable raging torrents. Water tore down the mountains to flood through villages perched on hillsides and outcrops, wreaking havoc and destruction as it went. Thatched tokuls, long dried out, leaked continuously. Pneumonia and bronchitis became rife, to add to all the other diseases of malnutrition, with pneumonia the cause of many deaths in children. Around the feeding centres a tarpaulin became the most precious commodity, whole families huddling underneath for shelter. Hercules flights were increasingly carrying full cargoes of medicines or bales of blankets and tarpaulins. One lift alone to Asmara carried

Gleaning dry kernals under a helicopter, dropped while unloading at Chisa.
Photo 47 Air Despatch Squadron

200 bales of warm clothing. In the villages a filched piece of air-drop polypropylene sacking could mean for someone the difference between a damp and a dry night's sleep. On the drop zones the gleaners struggled to separate the salvaged corn from the mud and wet sand, throwing it into the air to dry it. On village airstrips children would gather the few dry kernels dropped beneath light aircraft or helicopter during loading or unloading. Inevitably there were stories of farmers so weak from hunger that they dropped dead while sowing their crops.

*   *   *

Already, with problems compounding, a question mark hung over the future of Operation Bushel. Would the British Government continue this specialised type of support, given the prevailing difficulties? As yet there was no conclusive evidence that the rainy season was to be an unqualified success. In some areas of Wollo, Tigre and Eritrea it had failed to arrive. Though it was internationally accepted that trucking by road was the long-term solution, of the hundreds of trucks promised there were

many still to arrive. Of those that had come into use some had fallen by the wayside in the rough terrain and because of fuel and spares shortages. Floods only added to the difficulties. Traditionally Ethiopia had acquired its vehicles from Mercedes, Fiat and Volvo. Other varieties were not encouraged because of the lack of maintenance know-how and of spares, an exception being made of the British Land Rovers which were supported by a substantial quantity of spares and a British Leyland engineer-instructor who set up a servicing and repair base for the RRC.

There was strong pressure from the UN for the Hercules and Transall airlift to continue and an outright request from the Ethiopian Government begging the detachments to stay. On June 10th it was announced that the British Military Detachment would remain in Ethiopia until September 30th, jointly funded as before by the MoD and the ODA (in addition to an extra £750,000 for ground transport and 10,000 tonnes more food aid from Britain).

However, after a visit to Addis Ababa in the middle of July, Timothy Raison, Minister for Overseas Development, returned home in no doubt that the operation should continue to the end of the year. He revisited the Korem feeding centre which he had seen in November, spending a day at Port Assab and joining a free drop sortie. Concentrated talks were held between the UN and members of international and voluntary agencies, the RRC and ministers of the Ethiopian Government. It was stressed to the latter that those living in rebel held areas must also be fed and that there should be safe passage for food and distributors. But Timothy Raison was encouraged by the fact that the Ethiopian Government seemed much more ready to co-operate with the donor nations and was doing much more with its own resources (with 1,700 of its own workers in the field), in marked contrast to what he had found on his previous visit in November.

He told the House of Commons: "The RAF and other aircraft are concentrating on bottlenecks which are still causing most difficulty. The two RAF Hercules and their accompanying detachment have now airlifted well over 12,600 tonnes of grain and dropped a further 7,000 tonnes to places inaccessible by any other means of transport. It is an operation which, I have seen for myself, calls for the highest professional skills and cool courage. It is admired by everyone in Ethiopia.

Scenes from the Hercules flight deck. Water runs off the plains and falls into a canyon in the central Ethiopian highlands. Photo Stuart Reid

"The everyday relationship between the RAF and Ethiopia is very good. But if we are to provide long-term relief aid there must be greater meeting of minds. Among some members of the regime there is an attempt to concentrate on essentials, but the mystery about Ethiopia is what lies in the minds of those who ultimately hold power there."

So the offer was made to the end of December, a decision welcomed with gratitude by the RRC and with delight by the detachment, which wanted to continue. In fact the squadrons had been quietly allocating crew detachments for the next six months, despite frequent rumours that they were to withdraw.

Planners heaved sighs of relief. That the operation would knowingly continue for another six months greatly simplified supply which, until now, could not be rationalised because of lack of a known time-span. There were sometimes temporary shortages of items such as baseboards and sacks as manufacturers struggled to keep up momentum in the lack of long-term commitment. Now supplies could be ordered in bulk and the resupply aircraft loaded more economically with long-term equipment instead of bits and pieces. At base a large and efficient marquee-type structured shelter supplied by the UN replaced the RRC tents to shelter grain.

*   *   *

In addition to seasonal problems there had been two outstanding domestic worries for succeeding detachment commanders – the lack of suitable accommodation and sickness, much of the latter caused by the former. The very pleasant livestock research centre which had housed most members of the British detachment in the early days had been geared up for short stay only. As the months went by its rooms were needed for its own purpose. Incoming personnel were boarded out in downtown hotels, some better than others, with the inevitable consequences of diarrhoea or even dysentery. Transport from base camp to the various centres of accommodation and the collection by local transport for a punctual start of the day was another headache.

Few escaped the 'dreaded lurgi' (to call it by its polite name). Though the mains water was chlorinated there could be pipe fractures and cuts of up to three days, when water could be contaminated – and, during rare moments of leisure, folk tended to wander abroad for food and drink (though the local dishes were so highly spiced they were probably disinfected!).

It says much for indomitable spirits that there was little flying time lost through illness. People carried on working, often in acute discomfort, and if they succumbed there were always others willing to sacrifice the rest day and stand in for them, and much mutual support (one member of a drop zone party, taken ill on a DZ will always remember his sense of relief when he received a quick acting medication and toilet rolls, on a small parachute).

Diarrhoea could be violent and debilitating but was generally short lasting. Newcomers could be affected by the altitude in a habitat almost as high as Mexico City, causing insomnia, nose bleeding, tiredness and vertigo in varying degrees. Others escaped scot free. Then there were viral infections to noses and throats, strange bugs against which there was no inbuilt resistance. Addis Ababa was malaria free, but at drop zones and upcountry airstrips it was endemic, and sunburn and dehydration were real risks unless sensible precautions were undertaken. The heat of the sun during long hours on an upland drop zone could be very deceptive in a cool breeze blowing off the mountains, causing sickness and very red skins the next day. Airmovers loading or unloading at Assab, or people who were hanging about in a temperature of 42°C, could quickly be affected with heat stress.

Both the Luftwaffe and British detachments had their own doctors. For each current medical officer attached to the British contingent every day was long and fairly arduous, arriving with the early shift to purify water that was to be used during the day, filling the bowser from the tap, testing and chlorinating the contents. Everyone filled their own bottle which they took back to their billet. An evening surgery between 6 and 7 pm was held in the MO's hotel room with an average of four or five callers. It was also his task to meet the new arrivals with an early briefing to warn them of the effects of heat and sunshine, advising them on what they could eat and drink (to 'drink lots and pee well' but stay away from ice and the local bottled fruit drinks!), and the retribution that could befall anyone with an amorous inclination.

The MO was frequently asked to treat local civilians. It became part of the daily norm to hand out medicine to airport labourers for ailments from tapeworm to tummy ache, headaches and sore throats – a pill the great panacea. Anti-rabies vaccine was supplied and visits were made on request to Western embassies. Sudden emergencies involving UK residents working in Ethiopia or visitors were also dealt with. There were regular visits by the MO to city orphanages which had no medical assistance and various struggling institutions such as one run by nuns which 'saved' women off the streets. He departed from base camp for this establishment followed by ribald cries of 'save one for me'!

There had been a steady buildup of social contacts which had done much to cement East-West relations. On every hand gratitude was expressed. Some formal dinners were held in honour of departing detachment commanders or crews by the ILCA and the British Embassy, with guests frequently from the other embassies and agencies and the RRC. Many small hitches were overcome during a friendly social evening. Now, with flying interrupted by rain, there was more time to go down town, sample the local 'poison' (Metar beer!) in the company of the international flying fraternity and eat out at some of the better restaurants which were full of atmosphere and appetising Ethiopian and Continental menus. The famous 'mercato', the largest evening city market in Africa where almost anything could be bartered, was another favourite haunt, though off-duty airmen were dismayed to see the Lancashire-made sacks for sale. Had the original contents also ended in the hands of racketeers? The sceptics were convinced that this was so, that their efforts had, depressingly, been subverted onto the black market, that, in the words of one old timer: "Africa will never change." Others were inclined to believe that the black market was in sacks only, by a few astute traders who realised their salesworthiness.

Two sporting fixtures were held on the airfield. The first was a football match between the British detachment and the Polish squadron in which two evenly matched teams fought a closely contested game to draw 2-2. International soccer relations were further enhanced by a fiercely fought game between Russian and British teams. There was a record crowd and the British were grossly outnumbered, both by players and supporters. The match ended with a victory for the Russians, 2-1, with the competition and the height of the pitch leaving the Brits rather breathless. A downpour at half time made the second half more like water polo.

During July another major decision was made at MoD level – to accommodate everyone in one place, at the Addis Ababa Hilton, about twenty minutes' ride from the airport and considered by many travellers the only suitable hotel for transient Western stomachs. By the end of the month the move was completed, to the great relief of detachment commanders and MOs alike, who quickly found efficiency, health and transport greatly improved. The changeover had been accomplished by special arrangements with the hotel, at no extra charge to the budget.

By now Courtaulds waterproof polypropylene sacks were in sole use for air-dropping.
Photo author

CHAPTER FIFTEEN

When Life was a White Twin Otter

WHEN Canadian pilot John Hemstock and his co-pilot, American Andy Galloway, flew a television team in a World-Vision owned Twin Otter to the airstrips at Korem and Alamata they little realised the impact that flight, in September 1984, would have on world response to what was happening in Ethiopia. The aircraft was normally packed to the brim with food, equipment and medicines, its few passengers relief workers. After many months of vainly trying to keep pace with the famine they knew every nook and cranny of the two rugged airstrips. The hungry, waiting people could only comprehend that the "white bird which brings gifts from the sky" was not carrying so much food that day. For the twice daily flights of the little Twin Otter was their only symbol of hope, its arrival the high spot of the day. As Dr Jim Owens, Seattle based resident physician at the enormous Alamata feeding centre said: "When we see it we know that somebody up there cares about us."

For the two Mission Aviation Fellowship pilots, Jim McAlpine and Larry Nicholson and their other two colleagues, all based at Addis Ababa, the years of struggle against the slow moving agony of drought was so much part of life that they were constantly surprised that the world did not seem to know. Until the airstrip was cleared for larger aircraft the feeding centre at Alamata was just one of many where their light aircraft had been almost the only regular supplier. If for some reason they could not make it, there was a complete shut down of the

Four Mission Aviation Fellowship Twin Otter pilots, Canadians Jim McAlpine, Larry Nicholson, John Hemstock and American Andy Galloway at Addis Ababa. John and Andy flew the BBC television team into Korem when they made the renowned news film of Ethiopia's plight.
Photo Dan Wooding

centre where, on the good days, the staple diet was the small supply of grain mixed with vegetable oil, sugar and dried milk. They knew that each time they landed death was only temporarily deferred.

For Michael Buerk, then the BBC's Africa correspondent, the flights into the two airstrips were a victory against persistent government refusal to allow filming in the feeding centres. Only the dogged determination of his Pakistani cameraman Mohamed Amin, who was working at the time for Visnews, the international television news agency, gradually broke down their obduracy and persuaded them that there were advantages in granting permission. The result was a five minute clip of some of the most harrowing sights ever viewed on television – flashed round the world to 470 million people on over 400 networks. Never before had a small camera team highlighted so much desperation to so many people – shocking the world out of its complacency.

"We had been very depressed, for the rest of the world seemed not even aware the situation existed. We felt so relieved and privileged to have the opportunity to fly the BBC film crew to Korem and Alamata. The response was unbelievable. We finally got help", said John Hemstock, MAF chief pilot in Ethiopia.

The World Vision Twin Otter had been based in Ethiopia on a relief programme since 1981 when it replaced various small light (mostly single-engined) aircraft flown intermittently by MAF pilots since soon after the end of World War II when MAF was formed autonomously in US/Canada and Britain. The Twin Otter operation in Ethiopia was a joint effort between World Vision and the MAF, masterminded by affiliated Air Serv International, one of the largest private non-profit-making US charterers of light aircraft for relief operations, whose pilots have probably flown and landed in more difficult terrain than those of any other airline in history. John Hemstock (a veteran pilot at twenty-five – he had flown since he was sixteen years of age) had first flown in Ethiopia in 1983, living rough for six months at Gondar and flying fifteen missions daily to Arbaya, moving a total of 60,000 pounds of grain per day.

The four MAF pilots, three of them Canadian, had become something of a living legend in Ethiopia. Charitable Canada had provided massive support for relief, most of it in wheat. There had been plans for a Canadian Air Force Hercules to join the airbridge but a tragic accident on March 30th 1985 had written off two C-130s of 435 Squadron when they collided at Edmonton, seriously de-

On finals for a remote airstrip in Ethiopia. MAF operated Twin Otter. Photo MAF

pleting skilled personnel and the fleet, and it was not until 1987 that the Air Force did their stint. But Canadian philanthropic and medical agencies had provided aid in human terms, doctors, nurses, nutritionists – and MAF pilots. Of the twenty-two MAF pilots who were to serve in Ethiopia up to the end of 1985, nine were Canadians (seventeen nations were by now involved in the MAF, flying into remote areas in twenty-three countries).

Said John: "There were several close calls for us. None of us knew what could happen if the rebels seized our airplane while we were on a remote strip."

In spite of the conditions, accidents, though they inevitably happened, were rare. John Hemstock said proudly: "We had one of the best maintained Twin Otters in Africa, even though we had to work out of lockers on the hangar roof!"

All MAF pilots are committed Christians, inter-denominationally, many of them giving up lucrative flying jobs for the fulfilment of using their skills to answer a call of need. Far from being dreaming idealists, each pilot is obliged to hold the minimum Commercial Pilots Licence, Instrument Rating and 400 hours flying, and also a current maintenance engineer's licence on type, with avionics specialisation an added bonus. An intensive six weeks orientation course is undertaken before being

posted. The result is 'wrench and throttle' pilots with a proven track record for delivering directly to the point of need. They load and unload their own aircraft, and a typical light aircraft load in Ethiopia combined food sacks, containers of cooking oil or kerosene for light and refrigeration, mailbags, numerous small packets, vaccines and medicine arriving in the nick of time to give some merciful relief.

In January as the pace of the massive airlift accelerated, the crews were joined by three more pilots and another World Vision Twin Otter (the two aircraft were promptly dubbed 'Romeo' and 'Juliet') which was shortly followed by a brand new specially designed Cessna Caravan operated by Air Serv International to provide transport for more than twenty relief agencies in the country. Within six months two Air Serv Cessna 206s were added to the fleet, with a crew increase to twelve, providing transport for more than 100 relief agencies – aid workers and donors, embassies, churches, big industrial companies and the Press.

MAF pilots on routine maintenance of their Twin Otter after a day's flying, as darkness falls at Addis Ababa. Photo John Hemstock, MAF

During 1985 the five Air Serv operated aircraft flew a total of 366,293 miles in Ethiopia, making over 5,000 landings, the two World Vision Twin Otters alone carrying nearly 19,000 passengers. In May one of the Twin Otters delivered 424,000 pounds of food into remote locations, in an annual overall total of 3,783,876 pounds of aid related cargo.

John Hemstock had a narrow escape from birdstrike disaster. Flying at 11,500 feet above sea level over high mountain terrain between Lalibella and Combolcha, deep in the highlands, and cruising at about 180 knots, he was suddenly confronted with an enormous vulture. Just before impact it attempted to wheel, revealing an eight feet long wingspan, but in that split second he had the presence of mind to duck and fully deflect the controls, lowering the aircraft by about four inches.

Just missed the pilot's head. John Hemstock, MAF Chief Pilot in Ethiopia, had a narrow escape when a vulture hit the cockpit roof and shattered the windscreen. Photo John Hemstock, MAF

The second World Vision Twin Otter to be donated to the Ethiopian cause arrives at Addis Ababa in January 1985.
Photo John Hemstock, MAF

"It partially hit the metal cockpit roof, though it shattered the windscreen, sounding like an explosion. It could have come right through, taking my head with it", he said.

The aircraft was grounded for over a week while urgent repairs were carried out. It was a common African flying accident which caused a number of crashes and fatalities in light aircraft. Soon after, on take-off from Addis, another bird shattered the windscreen of the same aircraft while John was flying it, necessitating an aborted take-off. With some understatement he said ruefully: "I don't seem to get on too well with birds."

* * *

The role of the helicopter in any form of disaster relief is to be first on the scene with aid and continual day-to-day support. The helicopter operation during the Ethiopian famine was crucial to lifesaving in areas where no fixed wing aircraft could land, such as the many small outposts of human habitation clinging precariously to the mountain sides and those in deep and narrow valleys several thousand feet below. The helicopters also shared with Red Cross Pilatus Turbo-Porters the task of ferrying food from the delivery centres to remote villages, each with its tiny flat area too small for twin-engined aircraft. Traditionally, mission helicopters brought in fresh food for relief workers in the upland medical and feeding centres.

They were depended on for outside contact and health and well-being, on which the success of the camps depended. A delayed or missed visit because of bad weather or mechanical problems could mean that they too were on very short rations. The helicopters were also responsible for the transport of exchange staff and for evacuating nurses or other workers who had gone down with typhus or similar serious or contagious diseases, and indigenous patients. Collectively the contribution of helicopters was considerable, not least because of the dedication and perseverance of their pilot mechanics. The ability to take-off and land on small easily prepared plots meant that practically all parts of a given area could be covered.

Some Ethiopian mountain folk live a monastic existence in the central highlands, fighting for survival even in the better times, often two weeks' walk away from the nearest road, across country on which not even the sure-footed little Ethiopian ass could struggle over. Their meagre share of the massive airlift could only arrive courtesy of a half-loaded helicopter, dropped or landed, and the daring and skill of a pilot for whom wheeling and spiralling to avoid jutting crags or spurs in the path of some seemingly bottomless ravine, at the same time coping with wind shear and downdraughts, was always perilous. Low-flying Hercules crews could only ponder at each minute settlement clinging to the mountains, as they passed overhead. How could humanity survive, the skimpy efforts at terracing the steep cliffside the only

obvious manifestation of food production? The isolated farmers below could only wonder at the big bird's mission. Whatever it was they could not associate it with themselves.

When the rains came, provided that the shallow, precious topsoil was not washed away a crop was produced from hardy upland seed grain and they grew vegetables and tended their small herds of sheep and goats. When there was no rain they and their creatures starved and resigned themselves to die. There were no seeds, no grain, no animals and no hope. There was no strength left to cross the mountains and gullies to reach the feeding centres. They were the forgotten ones in a land where limited resources could be concentrated only on larger centres of population. Fiercely independent, resilient and inherently hospitable, since time began they had neither expected nor received assistance, and if visitors managed to reach them they were more accustomed to sharing food and shelter with exhausted travellers than to receiving it. When help arrived by helicopter they were more anxious about the wellbeing of their 'guests' than about their own plight! Reciprocal gifts which they could ill afford were pressed on the arrivals.

But for the efforts of some helicopter pilots who seemed to have an instinct for ferreting out these small

Lift Air's Bell 212 settles on a rocky outcrop – a helicopter 'pad' clinging precariously to a mountain side. Photo Lesley Hannah

'Miss Shirley' about to land on the helicopter pad at Shil Afaf. Photo Jim Gilchrist

pockets of habitation, many in dire straits would have remained undiscovered. Three such pilots, like the MAF Twin Otter crews, also became a living legend. Fellow Canadians Don Wederfort, Barney France and Grant Louden operated two renowned Bell 212 helicopters, 'Miss Shirley' and 'Miss Connie' for Lift Air International Helicopters on a mission financed by the Christian Relief and Development Association and the Canadian Government through '100 Huntley Street', a Toronto religious television programme.

Chief Pilot Don Wederfort, a veteran flyer of the Seventies famine, had vowed never to return after spending three months as a captive of Eritrean revolutionaries in northern Ethiopia in 1974, when he was marched at gunpoint nearly 450 miles (half of the distance barefoot). But now, back home in Calgary, the extent of the suffering haunted him and after a fact-finding visit he decided that armchair sympathy was not enough.

Plans went ahead in the face of conventional bureaucratic objections from the Ethiopian Government, with a similar experience to that of the RAF – permission granted while they were already on their way. Don flew the first of the two Bell 212 helicopters from Nairobi to Addis in April 1985 just as the 'small rains' were giving way to a full wet season and roads and tracks were becoming raging seas of brown water and mud, to start an initial four months operation which was to continue well into 1986.

Helicopters are expensive to buy and maintain and operational costs are high compared to those of most fixed-wing light aircraft, with a comparatively limited range. The availability of fuel in areas where they operate to most benefit can also be a problem. The great advantage they have over fixed wing aircraft is that they can be based in the midst of the action, and flying time, working time, loading and off-loading can be slick and efficient. The Lift Air operation earned a rare accolade from both the United Nations and the RRC as one of the most viable and cost-effective in all of the drought areas. The fourteen-seat utility twin-rotor helicopter with its Pratt and Whitney PT6T-3 coupled turboshaft power plant is ideal for the terrain, its range in the degrading high altitude significantly useful.

In these conditions it could transport between a tonne and a tonne and a half of cargo, of which 4,400 pounds could be carried externally on a cargo hook protruding from the underbelly. This sling system was the secret of quick turnrounds which the pilots got to a fine art. In suspended nets the slung loads enabled turnrounds to be accomplished in about one minute. A key to success was the basing of the aircraft as centrally as possible to all destinations so that all flights were of short distances. They varied from three to nine flights per hour, depending on mileage.

Operations were centred in two small upland towns in

Shewa and Wollo, Alem Ketama and Mehal Meda, 113 miles and 186 miles north of Addis Ababa respectively, both on the so-called 'all weather' gravel road which bisects the country from north to south on the eastern slopes of the highlands. At Alem Ketama US and Ethiopian Baptist missions had combined to build a large warehouse for grain and also helicopter facilities. The two centres served as a jump-off point for four of the six Baptist feeding centres where the RAF and Luftwaffe were air-dropping bulk grain – Gundo Meskel, Rabel, Meranya and Shil Afaf. 'Miss Connie' and 'Miss Shirley', delivering the groceries and medicines donated by the Lutheran World Federation and transporting rotating staff, became a familiar sight beside the Polish helicopters on the drop zones.

Expertise and a passionate belief in the cause brought the average cost of these helicopter movements within twenty-five per cent of trucking – at a time during the wet period when all tracks west of the highway were closed. The trucking figures took into account a complete tyre change every four or five trips of about fifty miles each, broken springs and half loads due to severe road conditions (when passable) and slow turnrounds. In the same period that a truck could deliver three and a half tonnes

(in return trips from eight to fourteen hours' duration) a helicopter could deliver sixty to 100 tonnes, with thirty four-wheel-drive trucks needed to equal the carrying capacity of one of the helicopters, and only when possible in the dry season. With supplies already centralised (by road from the Red Sea ports), the helicopters were delivering in seven days what the Hercules was air-dropping in five days at the same feeding centre. In one month the two helicopters transported about 1,000 tonnes of food in 188 flying hours, including completion of numerous, sometimes time-consuming rescue missions evacuating seriously sick patients or delivering food to mountain people.

One day, while delivering food to a remote hilltop village, Don Wederfort was told of a community of monks who were starving at the bottom of a ravine. The hilltop peasants had suggested that food should be left with them, that someone from the monastery would climb up and collect it. Peering down into the valley 2,000 feet below he could see no signs of life and he suspected that

Lift Air Bell 212 lifting off with supplies from Mehal Meda, centre of helicopter operations in Wollo.
Photo Jim Gilchrist

the villagers had invented the story to obtain more rations. He decided to take a look, making a precarious descent by spiralling his half-empty helicopter beside broken cliffs and the sheer drop edges of the canyon towards a sloping ledge about 100 yards wide before dropping steeply again to the narrow cutting.

Here was Ganamba, a tiny village of about forty people and, along a rock-hewn path, the grass-hutted, pallisaded monastery of thirty-eight monks. Once they had lived by bartering pottery for food, but now there was no food to barter.

He was to make several tricky descents into this wild, deep stronghold of ancient Christianity, flying in food, seeds (sorghum and barley) and tools, and he also flew in a medical team and later, Bob Geldof, while he was in Addis Ababa during his Band-Aid fact-finding tour of Africa. Don and the brothers became firm friends and at each visit he and his passengers were met with much bowing, hands clasped in prayer, and gifts of strange and beautiful bowls and pots of wild honey.

The vital contribution of the Polish Relief Squadron's 'Hip' helicopters has already been detailed, its transport of medical teams and clinics and the support given to the RAF and the Luftwaffe during the air-dropping of bulk supplies. The 'Hip' has its slot in Ethiopian history as a vehicle for good and bad – it was utilised in the controversial resettlement programme and also for much military to-ing and fro-ing by the Ethiopian Air Force and its Soviet allies for front line catering and ambulance operations, piloted by its Soviet crews.

Such was the enormity of the 1984-86 rescue operation that many northern European relief agencies who contributed helicopters during the famine in the Seventies were now using large transport aircraft. The Luftwaffe had donated two military helicopters and personnel at reduced 'rent' for five months in 1974 (delivering 15,000 tonnes of relief supplies), but were now using Transalls. Norwegian church relief societies operated Aerospatiale Lamas for eight weeks between May and June of the same year when they delivered 612 tonnes in fourteen different places during 480 flying hours, in areas south-west of Addis Ababa – and Swedish philanthropists operated a similar rescue package during the same period. The availability of fuel had been the greatest limitation.

Mission helicopters have always been active in the struggle for life, and another splendid operator which first surfaced in 1975 was the Swiss sponsored Helimission, then a one-man, one-aircraft operation by Ernie Tanner, a Swiss missionary who risked life and limb to

bring succour and the word of God to remote mountain areas. He continued intermittently after the revolution and by 1984 Helimission was headquartered at Addis Ababa beside the light aircraft hangar from where it performed some major and sterling work for the RRC with a Bell 206B JetRanger on missions similar to those undertaken by Lift Air.

As mentioned earlier, the Helimission JetRanger was at the forefront of Hercules air-dropping support, frequently flying the initial survey teams to find and chart the DZs and also taking on the task of transporting the British safety teams on occasions when the Polish helicopters were otherwise engaged. The five-seater JetRanger afforded little shelter during the long day on the drop zone and so the Swiss helicopter pilots built small shacks out of surviving pallets to shield the British safety officers from the burning sun, placing a couple of bags of grain inside the shelter for the radio operator to sit on in comfort. One morning during an air drop a sack of grain came flying, shattering the shack into pieces, leaving the soldier sitting on his sack unhurt. It was a nasty moment but it happened so quickly that he barely knew what had hit him!

Onward transportation of supplies by Helimission helicopter. Photo Ernie Tanner

CHAPTER SIXTEEN

Angels with Small Wings

THE previous drought and famine in Ethiopia in the mid-Seventies had high-lighted the use of aircraft – to save lives by saving time. Count Carl Gustaf von Rosen, a Swedish aviator and idealist, and his small team of Scandinavian pilots became the pioneers of air dropping in Africa. Under his guidance the Swedish National Committee of the Lutheran World Federation, in collaboration with the Ethiopian Red Cross, had been investigating different ways of delivering food by air and, in particular, dropping food from small aircraft by simple methods. Large military cargo aircraft, including those operated by the RAF, were already developing modern systems of air despatch but at that time they were dropping from high altitudes with very expensive equipment and parachutes which, to be viable, needed to be recovered for regular use.

Since 1935 von Rosen had devoted his life to relief flying in Ethiopia and was to continue until his death in July 1977 by a Somali hand grenade in the Ogaden desert. He is buried in the Commonwealth graveyard in Addis Ababa, his memory an inspiring legend of dedication.

It was difficult, at that time, to deliver food in bulk, and the feeding centres in the highlands were small and temporary. Country people tended to migrate to the towns or to struggle on or die in their mountain homelands. While helicopters were ideal for the terrain, light aircraft were considerably cheaper to fly and easier to maintain in primitive conditions. Von Rosen was convinced that, with simple dropping methods, their cost effectiveness could be further increased. Joint experiments were undertaken with Saab-Scania (which was developing the Saab MFI-17 Safari) to design a release mechanism and suitable packing.

Swedish Air Relief (SAR) was formed early in 1974, and the Safari became the first light aircraft to be specially equipped for air dropping. A pilot project of three months with three Safaris, SE-GHZ, SE-FII and SE-FIK, three pilots, a mechanic, plus a test pilot and technician from the company, were airlifted in a chartered CargoLux CL-44 to Addis Ababa amid some scepticism that the distributed amounts would be very small.

The Saab MFI-17 Safari becomes the first light aircraft to be specially equipped for air-dropping. Trials at Arba Minch, April 1975.
Photo Eric von Rosen

However, the project was backed by many relief organisations and by the Ethiopian authorities. The little high wing T-tail three-seat trainers had all the advantages for desert flying. They were tough and undemanding with good visibility and ground clearance, even when carrying an external load of up to 660 pounds, distributed on three points under each wing. If the trials were successful supplies could be delivered to almost any part of the country.

The SAR brief was to transport relief passengers and casualties, survey areas if requested, to land or drop supplies to the most needy – and to test the Safaris and their air despatch system. The aircraft were equipped with special underwing pylons where release hooks were activated by the pilot with selector and release devices. Various expendable supply containers were also on trial.

The aircraft were assembled at Addis and flown to Kombolcha airstrip in the eastern highlands near Dessie, the capital of Wollo province. Test flying started immediately and it was found that the bulky underwing loads interfered with airflow and drastically affected performance. However, when only two underwing stations were used on each wing and the load was reduced to 550 pounds to make allowances for both air-flow and the environmental conditions, the problems were minimised. Soon they were despatching very accurately on a predetermined spot from between three and fifteen feet (about six feet was found to be the ideal drop height) at an airspeed of seventy knots. The pilots had to learn to fly the new type of aeroplane and there were many experiments in the high density altitude to mix the fuel/air correctly in the Lycoming engine, including the best adjustment for full power, taxiing power and idling, with a careful monitoring of engine temperatures. In an area where fuel was always a problem, a long range fuselage tank was added. The plan was adventurous and successful, in fact at that time it was superior to high altitude dropping as practised from larger aircraft, which tended to scatter over a large area. The operating cost was eventually brought down to about one third of the cost of a helicopter.

The supplies for air dropping were packed in double bags, an inner bag of plastic protected by an outer jute sack (very much the forerunner of modern day air-dropping containers), after experiments with tractor tyre inner tubes which were quickly rejected because of weight and air resistance. Two double-sack bundles each weighing about 66 pounds were tied together and attached to the underwing release hook.

Air MULA pilots Dan Enhus, Carl Gustaf von Rosen and Eric von Rosen beside the Swedish Air Force DC3 tanker, donated by Swedish relief agencies, at Bulki in 1977. Photo Lars Braw

Packing in double bags at Bole Airport, Addis Ababa for Safari air-dropping. Photo Lars Braw

The first food drop was at the village of Bokaksa where an area was cleared of stones by schoolchildren. The approach was through a mountain pass and over a ridge which prevented visual contact with the DZ until ten to fifteen seconds before the drop area was reached, immediately beyond a row of trees. It was so successful that they were able to increase overall delivery from two tonnes on the first day to six tonnes by the fifth day. About 120 tonnes of edible wheat and seed were delivered to seven destinations some seventy nautical miles from the airstrip. To the hungry, primitive mountain people each arrival was a wondrous visitation from a world they barely knew.

Unfortunately one aircraft crashed, killing the pilot, caused by an attempt to cross a mountain ridge at insufficent height and meeting stall-spin conditions in a heavy downdraught. It was an accident which could happen to any light aircraft flying low over the terrain. Although the pilot jettisoned the underwing stores, it was too late. These pioneers learnt the hard way all about speed margins in high elevation areas.

The operation was moved to Soddu in southern Shewa early in June at the request of the Ethiopian authorities, but another aircraft crashed through pilot error and the third Safari needed extensive repairs after overrunning the airstrip from an aborted take-off – but not before thirty-two tonnes of grain had been delivered to hungry people. No technical defects had caused the accidents, nor had they occurred during the most critical time, when air dropping near ground level and at low air speed. Flights were resumed at Soddu in August at the end of the wet season, when seventy-six tonnes of grain were delivered to three centres. Overall, air-dropping had utilised 800 hours. About 60,000 people received direct help on 730 flights from Kombolcha and 170 from Soddu. The SAR crews were gratified to see that distribution was carried out by the RRC in a prompt and efficient way.

* * *

Air MULA (Multi-Utility-Light-Aircraft), the successor to SAR, was back in the field with five pilots for eighteen months from January 1975 to June 1976, after a fundraising tour by Count von Rosen, who again headed the team. There had been many valuable lessons learned. Now the problems were vastly different from those of combating the elements. The new Marxist-Leninist Government prohibited all private aircraft ownership and

Local airstrip workers become adept at underwing loading at Bulki. Photo Eric von Rosen

Local workers filling sacks with a grain screw at Arba Minch. Photo Eric von Rosen

Ernie Tanner's Bell 206 JetRanger inside the RRC light aircraft hanger for maintenance after supporting RAF Hercules air-dropping. Photo author

operation. Eventually special permission was granted, provided that there was close co-operation with the RRC, which had long had ambitions to set up its own air transport organisation – in fact before the revolution there had been plans for a fleet of about twenty aircraft. Now SE-GHZ, which had remained in Ethiopia, was presented to the RRC and re-registered ET-AFT. Another Safari, SE-FIL was ferried from Stockholm by Swedish pilots Gunnar Holm and Eric von Rosen, the pilot-mechanic son of the team leader. Unfortunately, during an early survey flight it crashed, again in violent downdraughts, into a river bed near the new base at Arba Minch, injuring Eric, the pilot, and a Swedish newspaper editor who was gathering material to publicise the project. They were rescued by helicopter pilot Ernie Tanner, who was guided to them from an aircraft which had picked up a signal from their emergency beacon. A replacement Safari was sent out by Saab and air dropping started again.

Before the operation moved in May to Bulki, food was dropped at Kamba, a small town completely marooned by landslides. At Bulki air dropping continued through the rain, fog and low clouds of the wet season, delivering wheat to five remote villages, in spite of fuel shortages. This was alleviated when a Swedish Air Force DC-3 was put at their disposal as a tanker transport, financed by Scandinavian relief agencies. Then the base was temporarily moved to Wollamo Soddin until the end of September and the little fleet returned to Bulki in mid-November. A new Safari, SE-FIM, was donated by Swedish philanthropists and immediately put onto the food supply of isolated villages, some of them over two hours flying time from base. A Cessna Centurion was also given to the cause by US and Scandinavian charities.

During 1975 Air MULA completed a total of 800 hours on mercy flights, on which 544 tonnes of cargo were dropped or freighted for the RRC. In January 1976 the base was moved to Tirgol by the River Akobi on the Sudanese border – a move full of frustrations. The DC-3, after relocating the team and fifteen drums of aviation fuel, broke down. Grain and fuel left at Jimma became contaminated and useless. At the end of the month they transferred to Addis Ababa, operating into the Ogaden on World Health Organisation smallpox eradication, essentially an aviation programme since the vaccine spoils after three days in high temperatures. Both aircraft were fully utilised. The Cessna Centurion (appropriately registered SE-GOD!) and a third Safari, SE-FIO were added to the fleet on the smallpox campaign.

Eric von Rosen, an expert on air-drop techniques, was now fully recovered from his injuries, and back in the left hand seat. He was able to repay his rescuer, helicopter pilot Ernie Tanner, who found himself and his three passengers in a similar situation when they got lost in bad weather and had to make an emergency landing after running short of fuel near the Somalia border. Eric found the helicopter after three days of searching, just when Ernie was giving up hope, his batteries so low that he dared use his emergency transmitter for only one minute every five or ten minutes.

By the end of April the Safaris were back on air-dropping, now based at Makalle where the crews were joined by a pilot and technician from the Ethiopian Air Force.

A flooded village in Western Ethiopia which received air-drops from SAR Safaris.
Photo Eric von Rosen

During the last six months of the operation they completed an overall eighteen months total of 1,488 flying hours, air-dropping or freighting, delivering nearly 800 tonnes, and also performing medical, passenger and survey flights.

In the complex political situation where all private enterprise aviation was forbidden and flights were increasingly stopped by security regulations the assets of Air MULA, including personnel, were transferred on July 1st 1976 to the air transport department of the RRC and renamed RRC Air. They included two Safaris, the Cessna Centurion, and a brand new light aircraft hangar built at Bole Airport which is still the headquarters of RRC light aircraft operations. One of the Safaris, flying under the Ethiopian registration of ET-AFQ, was written off by a bird strike two months later and replaced by SE-FIP. The Swedish pilots air-dropped intermittently into 1977 but found themselves increasingly frustrated by bureaucracy, not least by the Government's insistence on an Ethiopian 'minder' (security inspector) accompanying every flight, seriously hampering the load capacity of each little aircraft. Inevitably, efficiency was eventually down to about fifty per cent (fixed costs versus flying hours and transported cargo weight) of the original operation, amid suspicion of some corruption and dishonesty.

But the RRC stood the test of time. Indigenous operators maintained goodwill and enthusiasm, and by 1984 the Commission was impressing relief agencies with its hard and efficient struggle against famine, and sometimes against the obstructive ideology of its own masters, a brick wall for independent operators with altruistic motives who wanted to assist in famine relief. Among numerous owner operators from Europe who volunteered help, few were granted permission by the Ethiopian Government. The initial flight to Ethiopia was in itself an arduous undertaking. Few aircraft were allowed into Ethiopian airspace if they had overflown the Sudan, with whom Ethiopia was at loggerheads – and there was always the risk of being shot down by a rebel missile. However at the height of the crisis there were one or two, carrying supplies under the banner of charitable organisations, that did make it, among them Nigel Humphries, the Exeter based pilot owner of Air South-West, a one-aircraft charter company. Financed by townspeople he flew his twin-engined Beechcraft Queen Air G-ASRX to Ethiopia with a cargo of a tonne and a half of plastic sheeting, tarpaulins and rope for a Save the Children feeding station. He stayed in Ethiopia for three weeks, ferrying medical and relief workers to the feeding camps, and then limped home for necessary maintenance and to prepare for a similar flight to the Sudan.

Eric von Rosen with two Saab Safaris outside the new light aircraft hanger at Bole Aircraft, 1977. Photo Lars Braw

CHAPTER SEVENTEEN

Laying up the Stores

THE decision to extend Operation Bushel to the end of the year came at a time when some relief operators were temporarily withdrawing, either because of wet season interruptions to flying or because in some areas there had been a good harvest. In the south and immediately north of Addis Ababa the land had become green again, the animals (always the first to recover from drought) losing their rib cages and starting to show the bloom of health. For people the leanest, hardest time is while waiting for harvest. Many were still living on relief supplies but they were back on their farms, sowing and eventually reaping the first fruits, in an area where, in the good years, double and triple cropping was the norm. Around Alamata and Gondar to the west there was early promise of a reasonable harvest. As one RAF Hercules continued its daily landing flights and the other air dropped supplies in northern Shewa and southern Wollo, below them was all the magic of Africa, lush, tropical and gentle, the little eucalyptus-shaded circular villages surrounded by patchworks of green crops – as one crew member put it: "Little green farms – like flying over Ireland."

But further north it was another story – the familiar dried up landscape. Notoriously fickle in this region of Africa, nature had not been so kind. The rains had not been sufficient to produce a second crop, and in other areas, although the countryside looked green, the rain had stopped too soon and the crops had shrivelled in the heat without coming to a head. North of Makalle and in northern Eritrea, highly eroded and permanently brown, there were some areas where there had been no rain at all. In the west the rain had brought its own problems, notably hordes of destructive locusts or army worms which razed standing corn heads before the eyes of helpless farmers in spite of substantial supplies of insecticides delivered by the airlift.

To add to seasonal problems the RRC had turned its sights on areas of northern Wollo and southern Tigre which had recently been 'liberated' from rebel occupation by Government forces. The first RRC and international relief workers to enter the area reported dreadful conditions of starvation. Colonel Tsegaye begged the British and West Germans to air-drop supplies at Mehoni

in southern Tigre and Secota, over the Wollo border, both out of range of the Polish helicopters. There was an immediate survey of Mehoni by a UN team in the RRC Cessna including a detachment representative who charted an easy, flat 600 yards long drop zone adjacent to an airstrip in a sandy valley 5,680 feet high in the mountains. On a 240° run-in with a summit three quarters of a mile beyond, there were few tactical problems in comparison with some of the DZs already in use. But there were still signs of rebel activity near the chosen dropping area and no guarantee of security from rebel troops, either for a landing party or for an air-dropping aircraft. It was vetoed by the commanders of both British and West German detachments.

However, the Belgian Air Force, now at Asmara and gnashing their teeth against Ethiopian bureaucratic refusal to allow them to air-drop, came into their own. With their International Red Cross mandate granting them a comparatively 'safer' passage they were in a better

Below them all the magic of Africa, little green farms, eucalyptus shaded villages surrounded by a patchwork of crops. North of Addis – from the Hercules flight deck. Photo author

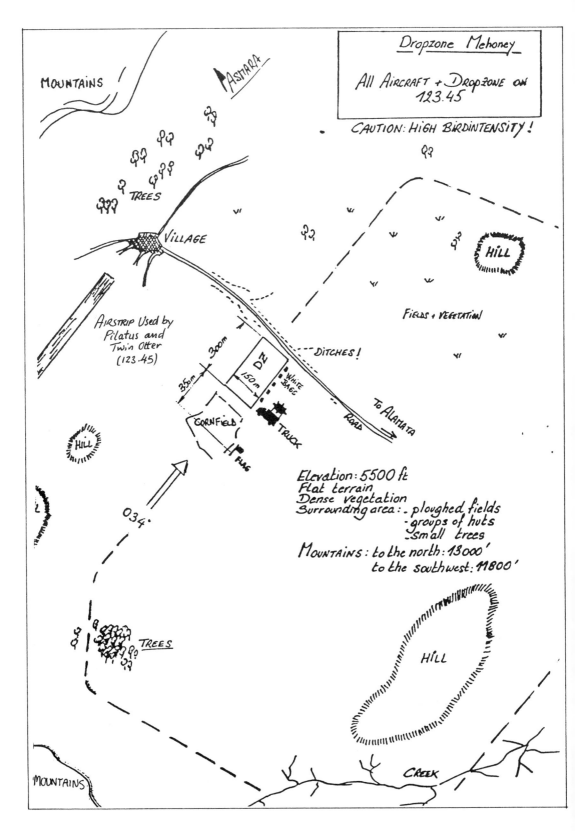

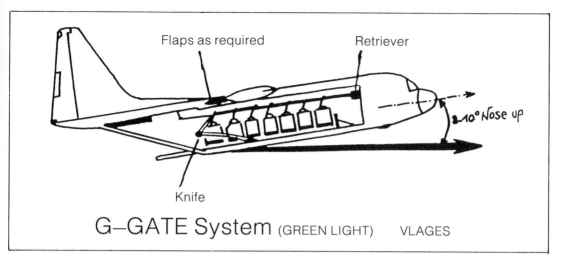

Flaps as required Retriever

2-10° Nose up

Knife

G–GATE System (GREEN LIGHT) VLAGES

The VLAGES (Very Low Altitude Gravity Extraction System) air-dropping practised by the Belgian Air Force and showing the retriever/ restraint at the front of the cargo bay, nose up position of the aircraft and the position of the knife which sliced through the back restraints of each cluster. Belgian Air Force

Belgian Air Force crew map of the drop zone at Mehoni, showing the all important presence of the Red Cross truck. If it was not there they did not drop. (previous page)

position to operate. Without consultation, they were suddenly told that they were cleared to air-drop. On July 4th they made a trial drop of over seventeen tonnes of food. After resurveying the site and preferring a run-in on 340°, parallel with the airstrip which was regularly in use by the Red Cross chartered Pilatus Turbo-Porters and Twin Otters, they commenced regular deliveries. Each Hercules load would have taken three weeks to reach the area in a convoy of trucks.

The Belgians had a simple criterion. If, after a low level recce, the Red Cross truck from the locally set-up feeding centre could be seen beside the DZ, they dropped. The driver, a one-man co-ordinator from the centre, cleared the zone, picked up and distributed the food. Almost without exception the Volvo truck was there. But if, on arrival, there was no sign of the truck with its familiar Red Cross markings, they did not drop. The inference was that rebel factions were too near for comfort and in a position to commandeer the food.

As mentioned earlier the VLAGES system of despatch

was unique to the Belgian Air Force, enabling them to drop up to sixteen tonnes on one run-in. A small team of Belgian paratroopers assembled the sacks on eight pallets (for Mehoni, one and a half tonnes on each pallet), which were placed in line down the aircraft hold with a forward restraint buffer at the cockpit end and a main restraining band which was equipped with a knife, behind the ramp. A static line followed behind each pallet with a small slack which, when tightened, brought the knife into action, slicing through each pallet's final restraint and activated just below the cockpit by a handle operated by the loadmaster. Three paratroopers, who had prepared the load, removed the main lashings as the navigator counted the seconds, leaving each pallet with just the one restraint before moving. The paratroopers were also there to deal with jamming or bags falling off the pallets.

Belgian made pallets for air-dropping ready for loading beside roller conveyors at the Belgian Air Force base at Melsbroek, Brussels. Photo author

Early teething troubles were soon sorted out. It was imperative to drop early and use the whole of the drop zone, and there was a tremendous trim change during despatch – a great challenge for the pilots. At first they tried dropping from thirty feet above ground but there was a heavy rate of broken sacks. They then tried more drop height and found, at 130 knots TAS, fifty feet to be an ideal height for their system, the vertical speed developing and horizontal speed decreasing. It was very successful with a high degree of unbroken salvageable sacks, the eventual failure rate three or four in 240 sacks dropped. However, their biggest problem was the ripping of sacks during loading and unloading by the roller conveyors which became blocked by the fabric. The spilt grain attracted the birds, large and small, and this constituted a real hazard during take-offs and landings at Asmara. Removing and re-installing the rollers every other day added another hour to the already long working day (including thirty minutes preparation and twenty minutes loading time for each load), but it solved the problem. At first polypropylene sacks were supplied by the British on request from the ICRC, but later a Belgian firm came up with a suitable two-sack alternative costing half the price, combining packing in jute and plastic.

Secota, fifty miles west of Korem and 220 miles northeast of Addis Ababa, was surveyed at the end of July, again by UN and detachment teams in the RRC light aircraft. Swarming with Ethiopian Government troops, it was a 7,800 feet high rocky plateau surrounded by mountain summits with a gaping ravine on the 180°(m) threshold of the 2,900 feet airstrip. It had all the hazards of the trickiest drop zones already utilised and some of its own as well, and seemed the most unlikely place to free drop.

They looked at first to see whether they could drop grain alongside the hard baked runway, but this was not a practical proposition. Scene of some of the fiercest fighting, there were still doubts that it was permanently in Government hands and disquiet that food dropped would not go to the civilian population. With no possiblity of an Anglo-Polish landing party and much obvious dis-

A RAF Hercules and a Luftwaffe Transall waiting on the Addis pan to be loaded with clustered grain for air-dropping. Photo Geoff Whyham RAF

Luftwaffe aircrew beside their tented headquarters at Bole Airport, Addis Ababa.
Photo author   (top)

Wg Cdr David Guest, British detachment
commander, discusses air-dropping tactics
with his 'oppo' in the Luftwaffe, Col Ranier
Westermann, at Bole Airport. Photo author

organisation a decision was delayed amidst some heart searching, for the need was desperate. There were no roads, and transporting food by a mix of trucks and animals a journey of weeks rather than days.

*   *   *

It was clear to all the heavy lift operators that to leave now would only prolong the agony. Grain, still arriving in bulk at the Red Sea ports from worldwide relief agencies, still needed to be shifted to needy recipients. In many areas the emergency was over, at least for the present. But now the objective was a positive one – a countrywide plan by the RRC to store grain in the villages against later food shortages, topping up the unpredictable fruits of harvest. Internationally, the momentum of air land and air drop was kept going with this end in view.

During this period the West German Luftwaffe had temporarily withdrawn from Ethiopia, closing down their maintenance base at Dire Dawa at the end of August. But they were back on October 14th with two Transalls, joining the British military detachment now that the move to Asmara of other Hercules operators had created enough parking and working space at Bole. It was planned that the two 'Tralls' would be concentrated on air dropping until the end of November.

The Luftwaffe set up tented headquarters beside the British detachment and also housed their forty or so personnel in the Addis Ababa Hilton. It was an excellent arrangement with a communal sharing of loading facilities and flight planning, co-ordinated by the RAF operations officer, the British despatchers loading the Transalls on request. There was a friendly agreement that, if a Herc and a Trall converged on the airfield simultaneously, the Trall would be given landing priority, the range of a number of Transall flights being very near fuel limits.

Throughout August the rain had continued, heavy and constant in some areas, spasmodic and unpredictable in others. More air-drops had to be cancelled. There were times when crews of both landing and air-dropping sorties had to fly as much as 150 miles off track to avoid bad weather. 'Local' thunderstorms could be up to 100 miles long, fifty miles wide and 65,000 feet high.

Even in the comparatively dry region of Eritrea there were pockets of weather related problems, as crews of the Swedish Air Force found when they returned to Asmara on August 13th, on request from the Swedish Red Cross, to fulfil a further eighteen weeks contract for the

ICRC. The narrow basilic rock and gravel undrained runway at Axum, at the best of times one of the most complicated of all the airstrips, was now inoperable. However, two days later the Swedes were back on the familiar three weeks stint, seven day week routine, their fourteen strong team (including crews) pitching in like the seasoned veterans that they were. Operation SWEALIE II/85 began with a first load from Asmara to Makalle. The Red Cross was anxious to concentrate on an airbridge to the dry areas west of Asmara and there were many flights to Gondar. Red Cross surveys were held in light aircraft at Shire and later Barentu, both strips with Hercules capability. Barentu, an Eritrean town sixty miles west of Asmara, was taken from rebel forces and fortified by an Ethiopian Government army unit.

Such was the confidence in old faithful Hercules SE-842 that it was once more back in the fray, with SE-843 staying in Sweden as the back-up aircraft. However, this time the old warrior was not so fortunate. Six weeks after returning, it was found to have extensive structural damage and was returned to Sweden early in October when Lieutenant Colonel Sveden flew SE-843 to Asmara for a six weeks stint on the airbridge, flying the aircraft home to Sweden at the end of his detachment. But towards the end of its stay SE-843 was to meet a moment of truth at Axum, now back in operation after extensive repairs and drainage by local workers. During a landing, there was sudden propeller malfunction causing severe yaw on ground roll and an asymmetric thrust during reverse. Largely through the skill of the pilot, at the time no damage occurred and no fault could be found after a thorough examination on the pan at Asmara in which engineers from all the other C-130 operators rallied round. The only solution seemed to be a propeller system change on that engine but as none of the operators had the spare *in situ*, the crews continued flying after a day's standstill. A few days later there was a repeat performance – at the same place, in the same landing phase and with the same crew!

A decision had to be made – whether to change the engine and propeller or to change the aircraft, in the meantime flying into Axum with extreme caution, using twin-engine reverse thrust after landing and consequently having to reduce landing weight. So SE-842 returned once more, shipshape and chipper, to battle on until the end of the Swedish airlift at Christmas. If ever a military aeroplane deserved a Nobel Peace prize for aircraft it was this one, though some British and Belgian operated Hercules, which returned again and again to take on the

Ethiopian airstrips, could lay claim to being runners-up. However, for sheer longevity in the field and overall bulk delivery a civil Herc, Transamerica's N12ST, would surely take the ultimate prize. An old character in itself, it was the first L-30 off Lockheed's production line in 1970 and promptly nicknamed 'Schnozz' after Schnozzle Durante when, in the red nose of Saturn Airways colours it first plied the airways. It was to return to Ethiopia again and again, firstly on Transamerica contracts and later for Southern Air Transport, long after most of the other mercy flights were but a memory.

*   *   *

Expectations of the southwest monsoon (when eighty per cent of annual rainfall could be predicted) lasting until the end of that September were shortlived in a number of regions north of Addis Ababa. The high plateaux in some parts of Tigre and northern Wollo and most of the lower plateaux in Eritrea did not get enough water. It would be a long, long dry season before the 'small' rains in the spring of 1986, with only an occasional local shower. However, the old familiar sunshine and come-play-with-me puffs of cumulus, sure signs of high pressure as the weather pattern completed its cycle, were welcomed by the airbridge carriers. Now they could get on with the job of delivering grain for food or storage without interruption or diversion because of low cloud and storms. Throughout September, October and November there was an added determination from everyone, whether landing or free dropping. The spirit of competition was still alive and there were a number of 'record' deliveries. Between August 23rd and September 11th Flight Lieutenant Alan Hill's RAF crew air dropped 1.5 million pounds of grain (the average was about one million pounds a month) and they were also the first to complete six sorties to the Adjibar East DZ in one day. They were 'presented' with a commemorative grain sack by 47 AD Squadron. On this DZ the Hercules air-dropped as much food in ten days as twenty-five trucks could deliver in two weeks (if and when they could get through).

This record was surpassed by Squadron Leader Jeff Bullen (on his second detachment) with a LXX Squadron crew during three weeks in September and October when they air-dropped 1,670,000 pounds of grain during 192 passes over DZs at Rabel, Meranya, Gundo Meskel, Seyo, Shil Afaf, Adjibar and Secota. Included in this impressive record was the drop of an inscribed grain sack at Rabel on September 19th to mark the 10,000th tonne air-

Trouble at Axum. Everyone rallies round to inspect No. 1 propeller and engine after a rough landing on the strip by Swedish Hercules.
Photo Ake Sveden, Swedish Air Force

dropped during Operation Bushel. Every air-drop sortie during that period was flown in Hercules XV306. Its belated flight home to Lyneham was achieved with an improvised pressurisation valve – a dustpan lid and four grain sacks!

During twenty-four days in October Flight Lieutenant Heselwood's 30 Squadron crew flew fifty relief missions delivering three Toyota Landcruisers, a generator, 537,300 pounds of grain, 125,900 pounds of rice, eighty-four pounds of high energy biscuits, 40,000 pounds of beans and various clothing to Asmara, Makalle, Axum, Gondar and Alamata. At the request of Ethiopia's President, twenty tonnes of seed maize was transported by RAF Hercules from Nairobi – a gift from the Government of Kenya.

Early in the month Alamata was re-surveyed by Wing Commander Guest and Flight Lieutenant Chris Kingswood, a 47 Squadron captain. They pronounced it operable for loads not exceeding 20,000 pounds. But the months went by and few of the aviators expected to be there much longer. Red Cross contracts were drawing to a close, and internationally, the urgency was beginning to centre on neighbouring Sudan which had the same problems of famine and war exacerbated by the enormous exodus of Ethiopians fleeing from their own unhappy country, a situation which was to get progressively worse. There was a general feeling, now that the immediate necessity of famine relief had been allayed in Ethiopia, other forms of aid such as trucks, road and rail repair and bridge building over gorges and ravines, were more practical in the long term, enabling Ethiopia to help itself.

Seasoned famine watchers at the British Embassy, in no doubt that the airlift had been crucial and had saved many, many lives, did not expect the situation to be as bad in 1986. The historic ten year pattern of drought had been broken by the rains of 1985. Road maintenance, though desperately slow, was improving and there were a lot of trucks, many from Bob Geldof inspired Band Aid, ready for the road and suitable for moving bulk food.

As one British Embassy spokesman said: "It is better for them to do it themselves. We don't want them totally dependent on outside air forces, but equally we don't want to leave them high and dry. The airlift is costing us £1.5 million a month. If it is not vital we would like to move into other areas and divert the funds to other aid."

The RRC were still begging the air bridge carriers to stay. Michael Priestley, the UN aid co-ordinator (who succeeded Kurt Jannson) said that the British Military Detachment had made a more significant contribution to famine relief than any other nation or organisation.

But in spite of all the efforts and the enormous amounts of food shifted to the famine areas, there were still pockets of starvation. Behind the rebel strongholds, and in spite of the sterling efforts of the ICRC and their even more valiant carriers, the condition of the people could only be guessed at. A poignant reminder was at Secota where famine once more became reality as Government troops mopped up pockets of resistance and set up their own military camp beside the airstrip. The ancient town and its surroundings, once the homelands of about 220,000 people, had been devastated by famine and war. Thousands had left for the long trek to Korem.

Swedish Air Force replacement aircraft SE-843 taking on fuel and milled grain at Assab.
Photo author

But there had been a steady trickle back – only to join their starving compatriots who had stayed behind. Red Cross, World Vision and Medécin sans Frontières relief workers, flying in by light aircraft, were finding hunger even worse than at Mehoni. Alamata, the only local airstrip of any size, was over seventy miles away and south-east of practically impassable faulted volcanic mountain terrain interspersed with gorges. It was clear that the only possible way to deliver food in any quantity was to air-drop by Hercules.

It was decided that the initial drop of food supplies would be undertaken by the RAF but, with the DZ out of range of the Polish helicopters, the question of distribution was still in doubt. However, prior to the first air-drop a UN/World Vision/RRC survey party was flown up by Colonel Tsegaye in the RRC's new Twin Otter for a four day supervision of the operation. Major Terry Lewis, 47 AD Squadron's commanding officer, headed the multi-national party and monitored distribution as an impartial witness, overseeing the delivery of 360 tonnes of grain and ensuring that there was distribution without interference.

He vividly remembers his first impression and the horror at what he saw – a ghost town inhabited by skeletal figures.

"It was like Belsen – only infinitely worse. The airstrip was in the middle of a military camp and my first job was to liaise with the army commander. We called an immediate meeting of party representatives, chaired by a small UN committee, and quickly arrived at a good working relationship with everyone, including the Medécin sans Frontières people who were running the feeding and medical centre and concentrating on the rescue of children who were not only malnourished but suffering from respiratory diseases caused by wet and cold. Without doubt it was the most urgently needed DZ that we were to use."

His stay included four nights in the small-town local hostelry – a mud hut at the back of a courtyard, wryly nicknamed the 'Secota Hilton' by its guests. When shown to his 'room' he found someone else already in the bed, who was quickly ejected. The living conditions were basic, with a ration of half a candle a day. When the evening meal was due, guests saw the animals slaughtered in the kitchen (at least the meat was fresh!) and were served up the traditional 'wat', a stew of meat and vegetables.

At the end of his sojourn in Secota he was able to report that food had been safely supplied to 15,000 starving people. The numbers soon swelled to 25,000 as people heard that there was food at Secota, many of them travelling for several days over mountains and valleys from as far as sixty miles away.

Though the initial control of supplies appeared satisfactory while the monitoring party were on the spot, the overall problem of controlling the DZ remained. It was obvious that only long-term continuous bulk supplies would combat the famine in Secota. It had been isolated from a more humane world for far too long. At Mehoni the Red Cross system of delivering its own supplies to its own supervisory staff had worked satisfactorily. And so the Belgian Air Force, from its base 160 miles north at Asmara, was asked to take over an extensive programme of free dropping at Secota.

The DZ needed a high degree of skill with accurate, gentle flying and dropping at the precise height onto the hard baked, rock based runway. On October 31st a Belgian crew made a VLAGES test run, the last pallets and sacks to leave the aircraft landing perilously near the cliff edge of the ravine at the end of the airstrip. Practice made perfect and they found the success rate higher with a lighter cluster and consequently they reduced each pallet load to one tonne for dropping at Secota. This still enabled them to drop eight tonnes in one run-in. As at Mehoni, on an initial recce they ensured that the Red Cross truck was in evidence beside the DZ. They operated one aircraft, rotated every three weeks, with a personnel of fourteen (including paratroopers), gearing in to an alternating routine of air-land on one day and air-drop, at Mehoni and Secota, on the next. From the early 05.30 am call to the 20.00 hours return to their Asmara hotel it was an arduous, challenging programme of four lifts, maintenance and loading for the following day.

CHAPTER EIGHTEEN

'Dehena Wal – Goodbye'

NOVEMBER 4th, 1985 – the anniversary of a year of continuous famine relief flying by the British Military Detachment in Ethiopia, with over 70 people and two Hercules based at Addis Ababa throughout the year. So far Operation Bushel had lasted ten months longer than any previous famine or disaster relief operation mounted by the British – and was still going strong. In twelve months the aircraft had flown 2,850 hours on relief missions and ferried 60,762,402 pounds of grain into the famine stricken interior. Now with the emphasis on storing, it was a vastly different operation from that which was started.

It was a year which would vividly stay in the memories of all who took part. From the cosseted West the aviators had come to help, a little bewildered that their fresh faced enthusiasm had at first been viewed with suspicion and at times even spurned. All returned home having seen for themselves what most westerners saw only in pictures – the dreadful results of famine in a world where deprivation was something a whole population lived with year in, year out, where life could be as fragile as a frayed piece of silk. Each man admitted to being profoundly affected by what he had seen and experienced, some said marked for life. But out of tragedy had come a remarkable meeting of minds among the most incompatible of ideologies which could only benefit both recipients and donors.

By now many servicemen were on their second and third detachment (and there were always many more volunteers); people who knew the ropes and were fast becoming 'old Ethiopia hands'. For Martin Towers, a young lieutenant in the 47 Air Despatch Squadron, his third detachment of air-dropping, surveying fresh DZs, and supervising drop zone safety was drawing to a close.

"I've seen all stages of this operation. When I first came out early in the year everywhere was barren. When I came out in July it was very wet and the crops were just being planted. Now, in many places the rains have stopped too soon. Around some of our DZs they have harvested one crop but the second isn't going to make it", he said. "Just about everyone in the squadron has been here, and we'd all be happy to come back."

At home at RAF Lyneham on November 7th there had been a parade of colour parties from the four flying squadrons, when the Wilkinson Sword of Peace was received by the station commander, Group Captain John Cheshire on behalf of the station. It was awarded to mark the four squadrons' involvement in famine relief in Ethiopia and for keeping open the airbridge to the Falk-

A year on. No let up as the anniversary of Operation Bushel passes, and labourers still hurry to the assembly point with two or three bags to keep the Hercules flying. Photo author

Col Tsegaye, RRC co-ordinator with the RRC Air Services new Twin Otter presented by World Vision, at Bole Airport. Photo author

lands, and the station's spectacular fund-raising of £48,000, most of it for Ethiopia.

As the last few weeks of the year went by there was still no definite withdrawal date, though 'before Christmas' was strongly rumoured. At home people were being rostered for Ethiopia over Christmas and the New Year. In the corridors of the MoD and ODA there was much heart-searching. Many individuals said frankly that they would like to stay. They relished the real situation of doing a job as against training for hypothetical military exigencies and continued to find the flying a thrill, a delight and a challenge in conditions which were acknowledged worldwide as difficult and dangerous. Lasting friendships were made with relief workers, embassy staff and many other internationals.

Feelings were mixed. Others, equally frank, were not so sure. They honestly believed that the Ethiopians and their Marxist government were, in RAF parlance 'a shower' who were relying on free sustenance from western countries while they spent their own resources on combating internal squabbles. There was an impression that, while the flying continued without interruption, for the Ethiopians the urgency had gone, that corruption,

far less in evidence at the height of the emergency, was creeping in and that it was politically right now to withdraw. It was felt that they could easily do much more for themselves and were even sometimes downright obstructive. Here was some degree of truth but, as one airman put it: "Tell that to a mother with starving kids." Even the most cold-blooded of sceptics could not fail to feel compassion for the long-suffering people in the provinces. Relief agencies and indigenous folk alike were begging the British and indeed all the big lifters to stay. Voicing the feelings of many, one Jesuit worker priest said: "Stay, and it will be the best Christmas present this country could have."

RRC co-ordinator Colonel Tsegaye said: "What the whole international community has done in this country has been a great endeavour. We have seen collaboration between all nations in the East and the West. Ethiopia is the only country in the world where NATO and Warsaw Pact countries have got together and done something great to save life. It has been the tradition of the military to make war. The reverse has happened. Here there is gratitude that the world had ears to hear the Ethiopian cry for help, and the will to make the first really effective food and grain transportation by surface and air.

"Ethiopia has the poorest road network in the whole world, and food would simply have not reached people if it had not been for the RAF, the Luftwaffe and other operators. We can say proudly that we have all done our best to make the life saving endeavours a success."

He added: "There is lack of seed grain and oxen, and in some places still food shortages. We know that the RAF operation is expensive but we still need them and would like them to stay."

However, during the third week in November Wing Commander Roger Green returned with a special brief. With his previous seven weeks' experience in the field in April and May he was charged with a forty-eight hours survey and submission of a withdrawal plan, pending a final decision, and offered extra aircraft.

"I indicated that as long as a quick decision was made we could keep the airlift going and gradually return equipment provided the resupply aircraft were the 'stretched' Mk 3s, leaving the current Mk 1s in the field", he said.

He made an inventory of surplus equipment, compromising between technical support and keeping the operation going. Spare engine, parts and props were packed up first in a calculated gamble that they would not be needed, a holding exercise until the final decision was made and the Ethiopian Government formally told. However, the decision to withdraw on 19th December was ratified before the end of the week, and a Mk 3 Hercules, delivering the last four crews and detachment personnel on November 21st, returned home with a first load of surplus engineering equipment. From then on, each of the Mk 3s was packed to the limits, in fact one aircraft had to wait for the temperature to go down before it could take off. The penultimate resupply Mk 3 left Lyneham on December 4th, turning round with home-going people and equipment, to be followed on December 11th by the last Mk 3 to bring in a final load of relief supplies.

The two Mk 1 Hercules, XV215 and XV295, battled on to the end, operated by four crews, one from LXX, one from 30 Squadron and two from 47 Squadron. Among them was Flight Lieutenant Paul Spears, one of the original four captains whose crews had inaugurated the air-bridge in November 1984. Now, he had flown in with a LXX Squadron air-dropping crew but soon found, as rumours of the final pull-out strengthened, that the priority had switched from food to air-landing large amounts of equipment, medical supplies, tarpaulins and cooking oil. On flights to Gondar, Axum and Asmara troop movement (in preparation for the Ethiopian Government's 1986 New Year offensive against insurgents) could be seen below. But the main task was the

Captain S Seuntjens closes down his Hercules at the Belgian Air Force base at Melsbroek, Brussels after returning from Ethiopia. Photo author

transport, section by section, of a large field hospital, donated by Italy, to Makalle. This was set up beside the airfield on the site of the original circle of tents which had been the flyers' first sight of one of the Makalle refugee camps. It was a major operation entailing twenty lifts.

Air-dropping continued from XV215 by the two 47 Squadron crews skippered by Flight Lieutenants Chris Kemp and Bob Rowley, and also from a West German Transall. The Luftwaffe, which had originally intended pulling out at the end of November, had kept one aircraft in the field with the intention of packing up the day before the British pull-out. But a severe birdstrike delayed their departure by a couple of days to December 20th while spares were flown in. Overall, during their whole sojourn in Ethiopia, they had lifted almost 20,000 metric tons of supplies including 5,159 metric tons air-dropped.

Dropping at Meranya finished in November, and then was discontinued at Derek Amba and Ajibar West. Only at

Gundo Meskel, by far the most inaccessible with as yet no haulage road, was the DZ used to the very end. Of those last days Paul Spears recalled: "We were all feeling we would have liked to continue air-dropping."

The last RAF air-drop took place on December 10th. Bob Rowley's crew made five flights to Gundo Meskel, and as the last sacks left the Hercules the loadmaster flicked the intercom switch and the sound of Band Aid's song 'Feed the World' came over the public address system. Hardened aviators and despatchers and Pressmen who were on board to record the last drop were all visibly moved.

During the final week both aircraft were concentrated on moving the final bits and pieces of the hospital to Makalle. On December 17th XV215 returned home with the two 47 Squadron crews and one from 30 Squadron, passengers (despatchers, engineers and movers and storesmen) and all the air despatch equipment and canvas. The empty spaces where their little tented headquarters had stood left a forlorn feeling of *déja vu*.

There had been many farewell parties. But Chris Kemp and his crew had their own way of saying goodbye to their friends – and Jim Gilchrist vividly remembers the grand farewell. His own stint at Shil Afaf had ended and he was back in Addis. While he was driving from the Ethiopian Hotel towards the Hilton there was a sudden 'almighty racket' overhead and he looked up to see the Hercules just a few feet above, saluting the Hilton (to the intense indignation of air traffickers at Bole!).

"They well and truly buzzed the city that day. What a good bunch, with great sensivity to the problems involved with famine relief", he recalled.

As they were announcing their auspicious departure and disappearing over the northern horizon the final relief flight in XV295, captained by Paul Spears, was transporting the last pieces of the new hospital to Makalle. Working almost every day during their last four weeks detachment his LXX Squadron crew had airdropped 1,400,000 pounds of grain and landed 116,000 pounds of relief supplies, flying fifty hours in the field.

On December 18th the British broke camp and on the following day Paul flew outbound from Addis Ababa for the last time. He said, simply: "I felt proud to see the beginning and the end."

There had been an emotional send-off party from old friends – from the embassies, Colonel Escheti and the RRC crowd, and many others. Local airport workers who had toiled alongside air movers and despatchers with such great team spirit bade their British buddies "Dehena wal", Amharic for "goodbye", with tears in their eyes. Among them young Girma, his future assured, but so sad to lose the friends who had teased, chivvied, supported and given him affection.

Wing Commander Green, his task also completed, remembers: "I thought we were never going to get away. It seemed as if half of Addis were there, not only the British expats – just about everyone, from local restaurant owners, the car agencies and airport workers – and even the Government news agency. Much of what we did was put down to others by the local media. Officially they appeared not to recognise our existence. But people knew what was going on."

The crew and twenty-eight passengers formed a big circle on the packed pan and shook everyone's hand. Paul asked Air Traffic Control for a final flypast, but the beat-up of the Hilton had been too much for them to bear and the answer was a vehement "No" and insistence on a standard departure. However, he pleaded a sedate farewell flypast over the airfield and pan, with a promise not to go near the Hilton, and they relented. As the four Allison engines thrummed their farewell to the waving people below, Operation Bushel ended.

*   *   *

From the setting-up stage to the end, Operation Bushel involved 2,000 people. Over 770 military personnel were detached to Ethiopia. During that period there was not one disciplinary incident. One storesman overslept twice. He was the only man who knew the location of everything in the spares department. It was pointed out that his action might cost lives and after oversleeping for the second time it was decreed that he sleep under canvas in a safari bed at the airport, on each night before his duty mornings for the rest of the week. Knowing his own failing, he begged to continue to sleep at base until the end of his detachment. Among the 1,200 plus who contributed but did not leave the UK, at the MoD and Lyneham, Upavon and other RAF and Army establishments, when the emergency broke many stayed at their desks long beyond the peak hours, to smooth the flightpath of the Hercules and see preparations through.

For thirteen and a half months (409 consecutive days) the two rotated Hercules lifted 32,289 tonnes of grain to the famine areas, during which for 300 days one of the two aircraft air-dropped supplies in thirteen mountain locations, delivering 14,439 tonnes by air despatch, with air-landing accounting for the other 17,850 tonnes. There had been over sixty crew changeovers.

Of all the bulk relief operators only the Belgian Air Force remained in Ethiopia with one Hercules on contract to the ICRC throughout 1986, spending much of that year air dropping into Secota where the numbers, swollen by people returning from the feeding camps to their homes and farms, reached over 100,000. They were selected by the ICRC because of their versatility and extremely high cost-effectiveness.

The Polish Relief Helicopter Squadron also remained, to continue their primary task of ferrying medical teams from Lidetta into the interior.

Ethiopian Airlines' contribution towards an increase in food levels was a successful application for a licence to produce, sell and service the Turbo Ag-Cat Super B for crop spraying in all the famine ravaged African countries, after sending twenty-two technologists to train with

Once more raising the dust as the rainy season ends. Dropping at Gundo Meskel.
Photo Geoff Whyham RAF

Schweitzer in New York. A contract was agreed with Pratt and Whitney for PT6-34AG engines which had adequate power for high altitude operations and the first assembled aircraft was soon put to work by Admass Air, an aerial crop-spraying company.

Also in 1986 the Wilkinson Sword of Peace was awarded outright to 47 Air Despatch Squadron for its outstanding contribution of air-dropping in remote famine stricken areas, described in the citation as a "heartwarming example of how well the British soldier continues to react when confronted with major disasters and how willingly he is prepared to help in a practical way." It hangs proudly in squadron headquarters alongside a Dakota propeller, a farewell gift from airport staff.

Throughout the year there was an extensive programme of major repairs and servicing to all sixteen RAF Mk 1 Hercules which operated in Ethiopia. Those that were used for air-landing needed changes of skins and panels, two of them having an extended stay with Marshall of Cambridge for replacement of cracked surfaces.

In Ethiopia, as the year drew to a close, a bridge built with relief aid was opened over a previously almost impassable canyon, which greatly improved road communications to Korem. A fifty-six miles dry weather gravel road from Mehal Meda on the north-south 'highway' to Rabel was constructed by 12,500 farmers in eight days.

The Polish Relief Squadron remained in Ethiopia ferrying medical teams from Lidetta into the interior. Photo Jim Gilchrist   (top)

The Belgian Air Force kept one Hercules in Ethiopia throughout 1986, most of the time air-dropping for the Red Cross into Secota. Photo Belgian Air Force

The land is green again, but the living not easy. Farmers take a break from hoeing their meagre crops near Lalibella. Photo Ethiopian Airlines

World Vision started its own sixty-eight truck transport company complete with parts and service depots, constructing its own off-loading and storage accommodation at Assab to circumvent port bottlenecks. The Ethiopian Red Cross also amassed a fleet of vehicles – still very much in an overall transport plan of trucks, aircraft, donkeys and camels. Band aid lorries got on the road and Live Aid pledged $40,000 to the MAF's 'Operation Flights for Life', increasing the MAF aircraft fleet by two and the pilots to fourteen.

Seeds for crops which needed less water were supplied internationally and oxen, given by or purchased from more fortunate neighbouring countries, once more appeared on the land.

In the history of Ethiopia there have always been three or four major droughts every century, and there always will be from time to time. The problem was not all the fault of the Ethiopian Government. But if policies had been different, perhaps half could have been avoided. It was easy to say and, even with optimism, difficult to predict what the future held. In the history of mankind, only the Berlin Airlift and the relief assistance by America to Europe after World War II had been more extensive. But until the big lifters came, everyone depended on the slow distribution of food, often too late.

Looking back, Roger Green summed up Operation Bushel: "We did a good job which increased our standing and expanded international rapport and co-operation considerably. A lot of Ethiopians were surprised at the Western approach. People misunderstood what we were there for. It was a fire brigade exercise. We went to put out the fire – not build the house. Relief was the immediate problem. We were there purely as airborne trucks to move food to where it was needed.

"Normally airlift is a short-term emergency measure of a month or less to stop people dying from starvation or exposure while ground relief becomes established. Nearly fourteen months of operation was exceptional. But it was the right time for us to leave.

"When we quit they had sorted out the big truck situation. The big trucks replaced us, bringing grain from Assab to Makalle and Korem and the main storage centres in the interior. The world appeal had been for big trucks, but they also needed little trucks to transport food into the remote areas. A number of relief agencies took on clusters of villages and needed little trucks to replace helicopters and light aircraft, for aircraft are very, very expensive. You know you have a disaster on your hands when aircraft turn up!"

Conclusion

THE crucial lessons of how lives can be saved and the basic infrastructure of a nation preserved by the timely intervention of international aviation with all its skills in bulk logistics were proved during the famine of 1984-85. However, it is impossible to 'conclude' where Ethiopia is concerned. Political pragmatism and a more permanent meeting of minds since the ending of Soviet military backup and the fall of the Mengistu regime in 1991 bring more hope of lasting peace in which to tackle all the inherent regional ravages of nature and legacies of years of war.

When the rains failed again, in 1987 and seemingly every two years into the nineties, much starvation was prevented because people were better organised. There was a gradual improvement of the road system, continued community efforts to build storage dams and buildings and some farming reform.

But the bitter wars against Government policies tore the country apart and became the main cause of human misery. There was no certainty that the lorry fleets would reach their destinations, and a number of food convoys were descended on and ruthlessly burned by Eritrean or Tigre rebel bands which were becoming increasingly highly organised. Nearly 100 trucks were destroyed in the first five months of 1987 by troops of the Eritrean People's Liberation Force alone.

Once more as a last resort, aircraft were called on to mount a rescue operation, in a concerted effort to supply people with enough food each month to send them home from the feeding centres and keep them in their villages and farms. In October Southern Air Transport started a single Hercules operation for the UN Disaster Relief Organisation (UNDRO) with money raised by the EEC, based in Asmara to deliver food predominantly to Makalle by L-100-20 (N521 SJ). However, the airline had already been approached by the West German branch of the Catholic relief agency, Caritas, to fly for its sister organisation, the Ethiopian Caritas Secretariat and accordingly, another L-100-20 (N522 SJ), adorned with the Caritas emblem, was positioned at Asmara before the end of the month, airlifting from base and Massawa and offloading at Makalle and occasionally Axum.

The forty-years-old Miami based Southern Air Transport were the first and largest freight operators in the world to use the civil Hercules, and after taking over Transamerica Airlines contracts and aircraft (including twelve L-100s) when TAA went out of air freighting in September 1986, became owners of seventeen. The SAT operation in Ethiopia was set up by Capt Asa Stackhouse,

One of Southern Air Transport's L-20s by the terminal at Bole. Photo Southern Air Transport

In Caritas colours. Southern Air Transport's
L-100-30 (N21ST), seen here staging through
Manston, Kent, broke airlift records in Ethiopia
with 648 lifts carrying 6,260,000 pounds of food.
Photo Southern Air Transport

Chief Loadmaster Garry Marsh and two service and maintenance directors, and masterminded from London by Calvert C McGibbon who controlled European, African and Middle East operations and had originally set the TAA airlift in motion in early 1984 for the US Government's US Aid.

"We minimised our profits as a whole operation", Calvert McGibbon said. "On a strictly commercial base donor governments would have had to pay another fifteen to twenty per cent."

Among the SAT team of twenty-one people, including three four-man air crews and ground crews, were a number of old Ethiopia hands (all loadmasters and maintenance engineers were former TAA employees). They brought with them boundless experience of the conditions and a deep involvement in Ethiopia – in fact four members of the original TAA crews had married Ethiopian women. Garry Marsh, on his fifth trip to Ethiopia, said: "Fortunately the UN had been there well ahead of us and they pretty well had things set up for us. We were ready to operate a very short time after we got there."

Following an appeal by the RRC to international donors, three Soviet An-12s and three Hip helicopters, permanently based in Ethiopia on the resettlement programme, were switched in November to distributing Russian grain. The Belgian Air Force was the first of traditionally chartered ICRC military Hercules operators to start airlifting grain from the Red Sea ports on 30th November, skippered by air-drop veteran Captain Peter Neats and followed by a second Hercules on December 4th. Safair, the South African carrier and one of the largest L-100 operators who had leased to Air Botswana

were also chartered, and by the end of the year up to five Hercules were operating in Ethiopia at any one time.

With conditions worst in the north, the whole airlift was first based in Asmara, though again, fuel shortages caused problems. The ICRC operation also included the three Zimex Aviation Pilatus Turbo Porters, the Red Cross Twin Otter and Lift Air's Bell 212 helicopter. On March 1st 1988 the Belgians were replaced by the Swedish Air Force, this time with their earliest purchase, SE-841 now converted to a C-130H with uprated engines. As before, the first detachment was under the command of Major Uno Haglund, and a three months operation was planned.

At first, much of the grain was trucked fifty miles from the port of Massawa and collectively the big lifters geared into daily movements of over 100 tonnes of food, feeding over 600,000 people. In April Southern Air Transport provided an extra L-100 for Caritas, this time an L-30 (the famous old 'Schnozz' now reregistered N912 SJ and liveried 'Caritas II'). It had been plying the Ethiopian airways since the early seventies delivering relief supplies for various charities. Before it was withdrawn this aircraft logged 648 airlifts carrying a staggering 6,260,000 pounds of food supplies, surely an all time record rescue operation for one aircraft.

But it was a short term victory over hunger. As freedom fighters on two sides overran more and more of the small towns and villages west of the north-south highway (including the holy city of Axum, which fell on March 27th 1988) efforts which were already hazardous and difficult became impossible with the Tigre People's Liberation Front maintaining a forward line only fifteen miles north of Makalle. Hercules operations in the north were temporarily halted apart from the two SAT aircraft operating for Caritas and now nightly based for safety at Addis Ababa.

On April 6th the Ethiopian Government ordered all foreign relief agencies to evacuate Eritrea, parts of Tigre and the major distribution centres at Korem and Alamata in Wollo, as a precursor to a major counter-offensive. After bombarding Wukro while Red Cross workers distributed food, it decided that the sinister machinations of a ruthless war were not for western eyes. Soon after rebel held Axum was repeatedly dive-bombed by the Government's Soviet Mig 23 fighter jets, killing civilians and destroying an Ethiopian Airlines DC3 so that it could not be used by the enemy.

The five ICRC light aircraft and two more Pilatus Turbo Porters operating for the UN were effectively grounded after being flown to Addis Ababa to hold until the situation was resolved. The Swedish Hercules, temporarily out of the country, was refused clearance to return.

The banishment of the ICRC in the north followed a gradually worsening relationship with the Ethiopian Government because it persisted in its mandate to distribute food in the rebel held areas. It received a peremptory order to remove its supplies, nearly 400,000 tonnes of food in warehouses, within fifteen days or transfer them and its vehicles to the Ethiopian Red Cross to distribute themselves. Suspecting that the share out would not be evenhanded, the ICRC refused. Much of the food had been undistributed because of the fighting but the Government claimed that it was 'rotting'.

Only the SAT aircraft were allowed to continue flying in northern Eritrea because, it was said, they were flying for the Ethiopian Caritas Secretariat which worked closely with local Ethiopian churches. Unlicenced to carry passengers, the airline sought special permission from the US Federal Aviation Authority to evacuate every expatriate from northern Tigre and Eritrea (apart from one Italian priest who insisted on staying with "my people").

SAT was also, at that time, the only airline allowed regularly to load at Assab for deliveries in Makalle and the north, as the Ethiopian charity it was flying for was autonomous from the Government run RRC which was delivering only in Government held territory. In fact because of this ruling the Catholic relief agencies were able to struggle on and distribute nearly a third of the food supplies in the country.

A nose job for 'Schnozz!'
Nicknamed after Schnozzle Durante when flying in the red-nosed colours of Saturn Airways and depicted here at Manston, Kent, this is Southern Air Transport's same record breaking L-100 pictured opposite.
Photo Southern Air Transport

"The situation became very tense as we continued to fly into Eritrea. But we were the flying trucks. Their people distributed the food", Calvert McGibbon said.

In Tigre, as the liberation forces advanced south and Government troops retreated into Wollo, Makalle became completely cut off except by air. The rule was: "Talk to the Tower. If you get no response – then don't go in." However, both rebel forces promised they would not fire on clearly marked aircraft bearing relief supplies, and they were as good as their word. But it was flying as close to war as any peaceful mission could get, a forerunner of operations to come in Somalia and the Balkans.

The UN chartered SAT Hercules continued to operate in Wollo and south of Addis Ababa and in July there was some easing of the tension. The rains which caused a flood disaster in the Sudan had come with a vengeance and a SAT 707 was allowed to operate a thirty day airbridge from Pisa, Italy, to Addis and Asmara with tents and blankets from the UN and the US Government's Office of Disaster Administration. A compromise was reached with the ICRC when it was agreed that the Ethiopian Red Cross should distribute food in the north under supervision from the Geneva based League.

Under the auspices of UNDRO, a C-130 of the Canadian Forces 435 Transport Squadron (UN 5400) flew in to Addis Ababa on June 3rd, to be joined next day by another Canadian Hercules from the same Squadron for the start of a three months emergency airlift called 'Operation Nile'. Bearing the blue olive wreath UN emblem, they set up a 60-man team (four aircrews each of six people and 20 technical groundcrew, the rest made up of medical and other support, rotated every three weeks) under the command of Lieutenant Colonel Ray Brown who had made a fact-finding visit in April.

Ferrying grain into the hungry war-battered provinces, the operation cost six and a half million dollars, and was financed by UNDRO and the Canadian Defence Department. On June 6th the two aircraft started a programme of four trips a day, while a third, based in Lahr, West Germany, provided a backup shuttle. Because of the fighting in Eritrea, loading at Assab was uncertain so, after delivering the first overnight load from Addis, they flew daily to Massawa, then still in Government hands but bustling with dusty, wartime activities and surrounded by bunkers and trenches. Much of the cargo was seed corn and agricultural tools carried in conditions from torrential rain to dry dust in an effort to keep the farmers sowing.

Aircrews from 435 Squadron, CFB Trenton's 436 Squadron and CFB Winnipeg's 429 Squadron each spent two weeks concentrated flying in Ethiopia. Though new to the conditions they found the hazards similar to Arctic flying! However, only four days after starting the airlift one Hercules lost an engine with a birdstrike, ingesting the bird into an air intake while on approach to Makalle. Fortunately the damage was minor and easily repaired. A later encounter with a turkey vulture was not so forgiving. During a test flight after maintenance on a nose wheel the bird collided with the port wing leading edge and ruptured a fuel tank. They landed quickly at Bole and evacuated on the taxiway. The backup Hercules kept the airlift on schedule while extensive repairs were done locally before the damaged aircraft could be flown to Lahr.

Team commander Major Bob Butt said: "When we got involved we had the same tasks as our predecessors, but towards the end things changed. Because of floods in the Sudan and refugees pouring in from Somalia we were asked to start flying to different areas, mainly points east of Addis."

Protective curtain shielding the flight deck of one of Southern Air Transport's L-100s.
Photo Southern Air Transport

Spot on! A ground guide directs a Canadian Air Transport Group Hercules to its parking spot at Bole Airport after a full day of flying supplies to northern Ethiopian airfields.
Photo Canadian Forces

Before they left, their Ethiopian loaders added another singsong to their repertoire – rocking the Hercules as they toiled to chants of "Ka-na-da, Ka-na-da!"

Operation Nile ended on September 7th after a short, successful mission by 277 members of the Canadian Forces, flying 1,100 hours and delivering some 8,000 tonnes of supplies. But donor countries were becoming increasingly unwilling to provide bulk food where distribution was uncertain and EEC and UN observers forbidden to visit even Makalle and Asmara. The Government erected its own iron curtain, with westerners effectively banished, imposing a permanent embargo on all news gathering in the war zones. By November only one Southern Air Transport Caritas Hercules remained in Ethiopia, with SAT already starting to channel its resources into a programme of locust destruction planned with various African governments using an ADDS pack (Air Direct Disposal System), a pod system already operated from Hercules on oilslicks with much greater scope than that afforded by light aircraft.

Although grain was still arriving at the Red Sea ports, there was a strong feeling internationally that only Ethiopia could help itself now and that the prior need for international aid was in neighbouring Sudan and Uganda and the time-bomb of famine and war waiting to happen in Somalia. The Ethiopian people had been provided with

seeds and the means to cultivate and the rains had been satisfactory. In a year when weather conditions could give optimism for a small degree of wellbeing it had in fact faded in the face of the brutal conflict, scorched earth policies and rumours of napalm burning.

As the year ended there were little signs of the 'perestroika' that was blossoming between east and west elsewhere in the world and no promise of a negotiated settlement with progressivly successful dissident factions.

But the outlook was not all negative. International pressure to end the 28 years war with the Eritrean People's Liberation Front was beginning to have effect and some degree of autonomy hopeful in other areas. The first Government efforts to liberalise its formerly rigid

One of Ethiopian Airlines' two new L-100-30s flies over the local countryside. Photo Lockheed

Marxist economy and to direct its resources from defence to development were starting to be evident, though too late to save the hated regime. Within days of the coup in Addis Ababa on May 21st 1991 (by a relatively small guerilla force), leaving nine million people needing food, UN relief convoys moved towards eastern Ethiopia, where starvation was rife, backed up by chartered Hercules. In spite of air force cuts, the Belgian Air Force started air-dropping food to demobilised soldiers in Tigre. Again amid great secrecy, the remaining 17,00 Falashas were immediately airlifted from Addis Ababa to Tel Aviv, this time by EL-AL, a night operation which could only be guessed at during curfew hours.

However, during the continuing struggle, one bright light at the end of the tunnel had been the efforts of Ethiopian Airlines, the nation's most forward looking of companies. It had long dreamed of owning its own Hercules to implement the transport needs of the country and had put in long term bids for two aircraft. This dream had been realised in July 1988 when it took delivery of two new L-100-30s direct from Lockheed-Georgia, after conversion training of company crews by Lockheed. The two aircraft staged through Marshall of Cambridge where they spent five days having minor rectifications and were painted with their new Ethiopian registrations, ET AJK and ET AJL, leaving for Addis Ababa on July 26th.

The formal handover was celebrated at the Addis Ababa Hilton on September 28th when Captain Mohamed Ahmed, general manager of the airline, was presented with a symbolic Super Hercules key by Jack Davidson, the vice president of Airlift Marketing at the Lockheed Aeronautical Systems Company where the aircraft were built. Ethiopia became the sixty-first nation to operate the Hercules.

The aircraft were acquired ostensibly for general cargo, and the acquisition was a major step in a long term plan to modernise the fleet, replacing two aging Dakotas. Equipped with high flotation landing gear to operate from 3,000 feet strips, they were suitable for use on many more domestic points than just the major airfields.

The advantage of having, permanently based in Ethiopia, the wherewithal to move bulk donor grain when it arrived was soon evident. Early plans to airlift internationally cargoes of perishable goods from Ethiopia, returning with vital products from Europe, the Middle East and elsewhere in Africa took second place to internal needs, though it was soon apparent that the aircraft would earn their keep when they were chartered the following January to begin an airlift of urgent medical supplies and food to war-torn Kabul.

The inaugural flight in ET AJK from Addis Ababa to Asmara carried 32,000 pounds of medical supplies and grain for the famine areas in the north, returning with 26,000 pounds of baled cotton. One of the airline's earliest contracts was with the United Nations, hauling 25,000 tons of food and relief supplies to famine areas.

At last, Ethiopia had its own large "birds which bring food from the sky!" They not only brought food from the sky in Ethiopia, but took their place in the international air freight and rescue scene, in a far wider ambit than just the Horn of Africa.

With 20 million people throughout Africa still underfed, those who gave so generously must understandably wonder whether the effort was all in vain. Those who took part, forever haunted by the eyes of hunger, whether aid worker, pilot, loadmaster or groundcrew, remember and know that it was. The funds were not spent just on emergency needs. New methods of irrigation, arresting soil erosion and reafforestation have proved that the people of the region have the discipline to continue the struggle against drought, encouraged by the agriculturally orientated Governments of Ethiopia and the now independent Eritrea, urging them to "grow a bit more than you need yourself."

In an ideal world no nation should have to turn to another for food. In a less than ideal world the overland transport of food is desirable because it is cheaper and able to provide bulk. In the real world of natural disaster, tribal conflict and man's inhumanity to man, air rescue, as has been demonstrated in Somalia and Bosnia, where hazards, though different, have been just as concentrating, will always be needed in emergencies. The experience, courage and selflessness of RAF personnel on Operation Bushel, the indomitable SAT crews, the Belgian and Swedish Air forces with their 'cut price' support to international aid, and the doughty operators of small light aircraft, are being called on again and again.